NOT

A

CHOICE

What You Weren't Taught About the Biology of Sex and Gender

PJ Paulson

Something we all desire, seek, and need in life is to be accepted as we are. Not as we "should" be, or once were. Not as we hope to be next week. Not when we've reached some as yet unrealized potential. But, as we are now!

PJ Paulson
Heart Connections

Note the paperback is printed with **Black & White** interior.

Paperback (B&W) ISBN-13: 978-0976323518
Paperback (B&W) ISBN-10: 0976323516

Except as noted otherwise, all images copyright by the author.
Cover image - Brain © Adobe Stock / Hein Nouwens
Cover image (background) - © Adobe Stock / deepagopi2011
Cover image (background) - © Adobe Stock / jijomathai
Cover color strip (if present) - © Adobe Stock / lavabereza
Brain (Front matter, color) © Shutterstock / miha de
Human karyotype (chromosomes) © Adobe Stock / Luk Cox
Yellow woods © Adobe Stock / Alejandro
Median brain section © Shutterstock / NatthapongSachan
Fetal development stages (B&W) © Adobe Stock / ngaga35
Fetal development stages (Color) © Adobe Stock / ngaga35
Base B&W Illustration of Brain and Head © Adobe Stock / pikovit
Hypothalamus © Adobe Stock / Double Brain
Hypothalamus detail © Shutterstock / VectorMine
Genes, chromosome © Shutterstock / VectorMine
DNA and human body © Shutterstock / watchara
Gender neutral illustration © Adobe Stock Viktoriia
Plastic bottles © Adobe Stock / curto
W-ROY-G-BIV-B Brain © Matt Astrophic

Publisher's Note: Reader reviews affect rank and placement in online search results, as well as eligibility for discount sites. To help others find this book, please leave reviews at online place of purchase, https://www.amazon.com/dp/B07XK8HKQT or https://www.amazon.com/dp/0976323516. You may send comments or suggestions via our publisher website: http://www.handselpublishers.ltd/contact-us/
Thank you! - PJ

Handsel Publishers, Ltd.
P.O. Box 53
Rush, Colorado 80833

Print version (US) proudly printed in the
United States of America

ii

Not a Choice *is a layman's guide to the whys and wherefores of gender, sex, and sexuality written in a language that those who need to know can understand.*

A book certain to broaden the reader's mind, increase our level of understanding of the fluidity of sex and gender, and our ability to accept others (and ourselves) the way we were created and not the way we are expected to be by an uninformed society.

Informative, entertaining, and to the point, Not a Choice *is a necessary read for anyone who ever voiced a question about the quirks and differences that make each and every one of us unique and worthy of respect, tolerance, and appreciation.*

Eric W. Brown, author On Beyond Yoga

***

This is a nice, clear, short description of the basics of sexual differentiation.

**Dick F. Swaab, MD, PhD
Professor of Neurobiology,
University of Amsterdam
Qiu Shi Professor of Zhejiang University,
Hangzhou, P.R. China
Head Laboratory for Neuropsychiatric Disorders
Netherlands Institute for Neuroscience, KNAW**

Associated with this book is a website that focuses on the whys and wherefores of being lesbian, gay, bisexual, transgender/transsexual, intersex, or queer/questioning, presented in a direct, straightforward manner: https://notachoice.net.

It also discusses influences on sexual differentiation in the developing fetus, including sexual orientation and gender identity.

You may sign up for a **free pdf document** containing a collection of the material presented on the website: https://notachoice.net/free-articles/

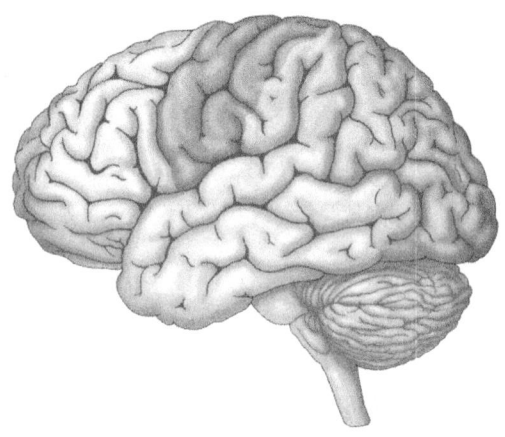

A simple signup page to be notified of future research discoveries in this field is here.

A Note from the Author

When I began my university education, it was as a biology major, with the intent of enjoying a lifelong career in genetics research. I wound up as a software engineer. The summer of 2019, I put my love of genetics and research to work, and pored through 30 years of books, reports, and scientific publications to expand on what I had read years before about the biological basis of femaleness versus maleness, gender identity, and sexual orientation. The result was a book written in layman's terms intended to educate the general public and lawmakers. That book is *Not a Choice: What you weren't taught about the biology of sex and gender.*

The information contained in *Not a Choice* and on the https://notachoice.net website is important for all of us to know and to understand at least on a basic level. A large amount of complex technical research findings has been distilled to an everyday read in fairly plain English. The extensive list of references has been provided on the website as well as in *Not a Choice* in order to demonstrate its solid foundation.

Our mission is to improve self-acceptance and acceptance of others in a large proportion of the world's population. I welcome you as part of that effort.

PJ Paulson
February 4, 2021

Disclaimer

The ideas expressed in this book are sourced from books and research materials published by scientists and medical professionals. Author opinions expressed in accompanying commentary should not be considered authoritative or professional statements; the author is not a professional in the fields of biology, counseling and/or psychology. This book is provided with the intent that the stories and ideas presented herein may widen the scope of the readers' thought processes, acceptance of themselves, and acceptance of those different from themselves.

This book is sold with the understanding that the author and publisher are not performing legal or professional services. If expert assistance is required, the services of a competent professional should be sought.

The purpose of this book is to educate and to entertain. Every effort has been made to make this book as complete and as accurate as possible. However, there may be mistakes, either in typography or in content. New information becomes available as research continues; a lag may occur between the time of publication of that new material and updates to this book. The author and the publisher shall have neither liability nor responsibility to any person or entity with respect to any loss or damage caused or alleged to have been caused, directly or indirectly, by any information contained in this book.

Preface

The facts presented in this book may be new to many of you. They are not cockamamie ideas made up by peddlers of snake-oil. I was first introduced to them in the early 1990s when I read a book by Anne Moir and David Jessel. I never was crazy about the title *Brain Sex: The real difference between Men & Women*, but I thought it was a great book.

What stuck with me over nearly three decades was that it explained in straightforward terms the combination of genetics and fetal exposure to hormones (or lack of) in determining sex, physical appearance of sex, male versus female brain structure (and function), and gender identity. Studies and research that provided the foundation work for the book were extensive; references listed for a single chapter may run several pages.

My paperback copy with the yellow highlighting and handwritten margin notes was loaned to a friend and then lost. Years later I replaced it with a hardbound copy, which I planned to use as a reference for this book, but I didn't know if its content had held up over the years. When I began researching, it appeared that the information provided in Moir and Jessel's book still was not widely known. Yet, I found multiple additional reputable sources stating the same, now scientifically accepted, facts.

One of these sources is an article by Bruce Goldman published in 2017 by Stanford Medicine. In it he states the following:

> Over the past 15 years or so, there's been a sea change as new technologies have generated a growing pile of evidence that there are inherent differences in how men's and women's brains are wired and how they work.
> ... Our differences don't mean one sex or the other is better or smarter or more deserving.... Data from animal research, cross-cultural surveys, natural experiments and brain-imaging studies demonstrate real, if not always earthshaking, brain differences, and that these differences may contribute to differences in behavior and cognition.

One of Goldman's sources was Diane Halpern, PhD, whom Goldman cites as past president of the American Psychological Association and author of *Sex Differences in Cognitive Abilities.*

Goldman says of Halpern:

> [In 1991] she found that the animal-research literature had been steadily accreting reports of sex-associated neuroanatomical and behavioral differences, but those studies were mainly gathering dust in university libraries. Social psychologists and sociologists pooh-poohed the notion of any fundamental cognitive differences between male and female humans, notes Halpern, a professor emerita of psychology at Claremont McKenna College.

> In her preface to the first edition, Halpern wrote: "At the time, it seemed clear to me that any between-sex differences in thinking abilities were due to socialization practices, artifacts and mistakes in the research, and bias and prejudice. ... After reviewing a pile of journal articles

that stood several feet high and numerous books and book chapters that dwarfed the stack of journal articles ... I changed my mind."

Why? There was too much data pointing to the biological basis of sex-based cognitive differences to ignore, Halpern says.

This book does not include re-hashing the merit of facts that have become established among the scientific community, albeit perhaps not well-known among the general population. Nor am I attempting to convince readers of the validity of the research behind the material presented.

With studies in this field ongoing, available information changes over time. What is included here is quite well established among researchers at the time of this writing. The resources providing the basis for this book support one another, and have been published by highly-respected institutions and individuals. Though research in genetics, endocrinology, and brain structure and function continue, all attempts have been made to present what is currently known with the utmost integrity.

The author of two books and lead researcher on several papers among my resources is Dick Swaab, a physician, neurobiologist, professor of neurobiology at the University of Amsterdam, and was for 27 years Director of the Netherlands Institute for Brain Research of the Royal Netherlands Academy of Arts and Sciences. He is an internationally renowned researcher in the field of neuroscience, and has published two books for the general public, several for the scientific community, and hundreds of research papers. In his book *Our Creative Brains: How World and Mankind Shape Each Other*, Dr. Swaab stresses the presence and acceptance of evidence for sexual differentiation in certain structures within the human brain and consequent variations in sex-related brain structure and function.

> Biology has amassed a great deal of experimental and clinical data about the programming effects of the Y chromosome and the male hormone testosterone on the development of the brains of male embryos in the second half of pregnancy. Already at that stage there are molecular differences between male and female brains. Sex-based differences in many brain structures and behaviours at the level of men and women as groups are now well documented.

My goal with this book is simply to create a short, plainly-stated, easy-to-understand presentation of the biological bases for the complex expressions of sex and gender. Toward that goal, the later discussion of genetic conditions involving sex chromosomes will not include medical symptoms or complications beyond those immediately relevant to sex and gender.

My hope is that once understood, all configurations and expressions will more readily be accepted.

Table of Contents

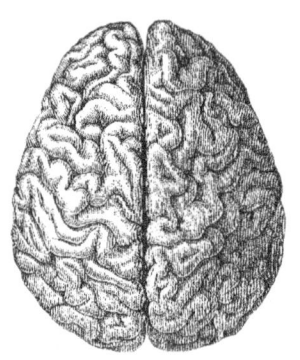

Introduction

Why this book? Why this topic?

It's hard to believe that more than thirty years after publication of findings on the complexity of sex and gender, there are very few people who are aware of it. There are biological bases for the differences between women and men, as well as for a complex set of alternatives not fully fitting either of those binary categories. Though the possibilities are varied, they're fairly simple to understand.

It pains me to hear of people who struggle with their own gender identity or sexual orientation. It's tragic that such struggles can lead to suicide or attempted suicide.

Why are discriminatory and even violent acts still in the news against LGBTQ individuals and groups? Haven't we grown beyond persecuting those who may be perceived as different? In the words of Dick Swaab, "We are all different. Variation was the motor of the evolution, and the variation is still present in all our systems, including those involved in gender identity and sexual orientation." (Commentary on *Not a Choice*, October 29, 2019.)

It's more practical to embrace one another's differences. If everyone were the same, we might all be auto workers. There would be plenty of new cars, but if everyone built cars and there were no farmers, we all would starve. We cannot all be the same and survive, either as a society or as individuals. Give that some consideration.

When prejudices attempt to taint our politics and court rulings in favor of discrimination, what rabbit hole have we as a nation fallen down?

My two reasons for writing about this topic are these:

1) To educate political leaders, lawmakers, and the regular Joe and Joan on the street that sex is much more complex than the simple female-male binary system we've been taught. Multiple paths may lead to multiple results. LGBTQ people, just like heterosexual female and heterosexual male individuals, are living as directed by their genetics, brain structure, and hormones. It's biological for us all.

2) To help those struggling with their own gender identity to understand that there is nothing inherently "wrong" with them that necessitates feelings of guilt.

No-one should have to explain to anyone else the biology behind their genetic sex, gender identity, or sexual preference. That said, if more people were informed of and understood the variations that can and do exist, mightn't they be more accepting of both themselves and of those different from themselves?

Please keep an open mind and digest what you read here.

A note on terminology

For the most part, layman's terms are used, in which meaning is known or can be easily understood. For example, brain "dimorphism" means that the brain morphs, or differentiates, into two distinct forms – either male or female. In reality, that's an oversimplification – different areas of the brain develop to differing degrees as male or female, creating a **mosaic** of both female and male patterning in each person.

Dick Swaab explains this mosaic in *Our Creative Brains*:

> A given individual does not simply have either a male or a female brain, or display either male or female behaviour. Each has a unique mosaic of more or less male or female characteristics. There is therefore great variety in the sexual differentiation of brain systems even within one and the same person.

(Dick Swaab, *Our Creative Brains: How World and Mankind Shape Each Other,* III.1. Sexual differentiation of the brain, 2019.)

Terms "sex" and "gender" are not used to mean the same concept, and are not interchangeable.

"Sex" generally will be used for representation based on genetic sex chromosomes, and is commonly used in reference to the sexual appearance of genitals; think male versus female.

"Gender" will be used primarily in the context of gender identity – man versus woman, or the *feeling* of being male versus female.

"Gender identity" refers to how a person self-identifies on the male-female spectrum; the degree to which they feel themselves as male-female. The brain mosaic may or may not lead to distinct feelings of maleness or femaleness.

"Sexual orientation" is used in regard to an individual's partner selection, and should not be confused with gender identity.

"LGBTQ" stands for Lesbian, Gay, Bisexual, Transgender, and Queer or Questioning. "I" (as in LGBTQI) stands for Intersex (see below).

"Intersex" often refers to physical appearance of genitals, but may be used in broader terms of non-binary sexual differentiation such as gender identity or sexual orientation. Intersex individuals represent as much as two percent of the world population – about as many people as those having naturally red hair.

"Mosaic" versus "Dimorphic" brain patterning
Scientific literature is moving away from the concept of general male-female brain dimorphism toward the term "mosaic," which more precisely describes the differences between female and male brain structures.

As explained by Daphna Joel, true dimorphism in the context of brain development would imply (1) very little overlap between the structure of a male brain and a female brain, taken as a whole, and (2) internal consistency, meaning that a brain would contain only or predominantly either male or female features. Neither of these is the case (Joel et al., 2015).

The reality is that there are several structures within the human brain that have been found to differ in size and function between the general male population and general female population.

Just as men produce predominantly male hormones with very small amounts of female hormones, and women produce predominantly female hormones with small amounts of male hormones, the brain structures lean predominantly toward male or female. That is, the brain structures that normally differentiate based on sex, taken all together in an individual, will lean toward either male or female, with lesser amounts leaning in the other direction. It is very, very rare for an individual's sexually-differentiated brain structures to all follow a male pattern or all follow a female pattern (Joel et al., 2015).

Keeping this in mind, simple terms such as "female patterning," "female-patterned versus male-patterned," or "male development" may be used in this book to describe the *overall* direction in which the brain is patterned, female versus male.

While more extreme measures can be taken in studies on rats and mice, in humans the most readily measurable attributes (via MRI or in donated brain tissue) are the volume, density, and size of a particular brain area. Then functional MRIs (fMRI) in live subjects can correlate responses in specific brain areas with external stimuli.

Neuronal cell counts, density, and volume of a specific structure occur over a range. While it's possible to determine with 80% accuracy, or better, the sex of a person based on measurements of a set of these differentiated brain structures, the brain considered as a whole does not meet the two criteria specified to be truly dimorphic. It is not the entire brain that develops into an identifiable female or male pattern. And there is some overlap in the measurable attributes of the structures that are known to differentiate as male versus female.

What we have, then, is a brain containing a number of structures known to differentiate in male versus female patterning. Most of these structures appear to develop at different times and independently of one another, and can exhibit different degrees of maleness or femaleness. It's a spectrum of possibilities rather than binary, either-or, development.

The femaleness or maleness of a brain, then, is presented in a mosaic of brain structures, each of which has differentiated to some degree into a female or male pattern.

Presentation

We'll begin with a brief refresher on the most elemental aspects of biology and genetics as related to sex determination.

Once we understand the basics, we'll talk about male-female brain and behavioral differences. It's important to understand that differences in brain structure drive real differences in function, preferences, strengths, and behavior over the female-male continuum.

Then, we'll explore the paths that fetal development can take both in and beyond the binary "norm" we've likely been taught. The reality is an actual non-binary journey creating mosaic results to varying degrees of both maleness and femaleness in all of us.

Note: It should be noted that males produce small amounts of female hormones, and females produce small amounts of male hormones. These low levels of opposite-sex hormones have been considered insubstantial in most discussions of male-female differentiation in the literature I have read. However, I have to think it's likely that they play a role in the findings that it is extremely rare for the currently-known sexually differentiated structures of the brain to all follow either male patterning or female patterning – they almost always present a mosaic comprised of both.

A Biology Refresher

A normal human body possesses 23 pair of chromosomes, for a total of 46. Twenty-two of these pair are the "regular" chromosomes, known as "autosomes." In addition, there is one set of chromosomes that determines a person's sex. Under usual circumstances, this set is a pair consisting of either two X chromosomes (female), or one X and one Y (male). However, there are not always 2 sex chromosomes present.

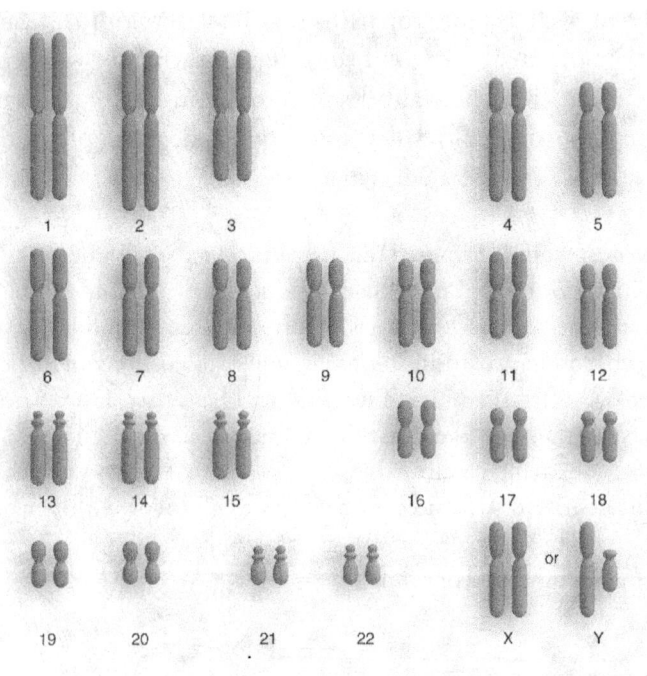

Human karyotype (chromosomes) © Adobe Stock / Luk Cox

How does this work?

A child inherits 23 chromosomes from each of its parents, for a total of 46. Combined in the child, these make up the 22 pair of autosomes and one pair of sex chromosomes. Sex chromosomes are known as "X" and "Y" and together determine the genetic sex of the child.

Under normal circumstances, each parent donates a single sex chromosome to the offspring.

Along with the other 22 chromosomes she contributes to the child, the mother's egg contains one X sex chromosome. A child will inherit this chromosome from their mother.

Along with the other 22 chromosomes the father contributes to the child, the father's sperm each may contain either an X sex chromosome or a Y sex chromosome. If a sperm containing an X sex chromosome fertilizes the egg, the child will have two X sex chromosomes, and be a genetic female (XX). If a sperm containing a Y sex chromosome fertilizes the egg, the child will have one X sex chromosome (from the mother) and one Y sex chromosome (from the father), and be a genetic male (XY).

Each child has a roughly 50% chance of being a girl and a 50% chance of being a boy. Interesting note: there are about 1,500 genes on an X chromosome, and sources have estimates ranging from about 27 to more than 200 on the Y (NCBI, "Genes and Disease," 2011).

X and Y chromosome history, discovery, and naming

Wikipedia reports that the notion of X and Y chromosomes being named for their shape is false.

Our XY system of sex chromosomes in mammals is believed to have originated from a pair of autosomes millions of years ago. While earlier estimates placed X and Y chromosome emergence in the pre-human line at 300 million years ago, more recent estimates place it at 160 million years ago, when monotremes (e.g., platypus and echidna) split from other mammals.

While the X exhibits more stability, the Y chromosome is believed to have lost most of its genes prior to human divergence from non-human primates six to seven million years ago. It has maintained its gene content since that divergence. A 2012 report goes further back, saying that only one gene has been lost since the pre-human line diverged from rhesus macaques 25 million years ago.

The X chromosome was identified in 1890 by Hermann Henking. According to Wikipedia's "Hermann Henking" article (Wikipedia, "Hermann Henking," June 14, 2017), Henking was studying testicles of the firebug in Leipzig when he noticed a chromosome that did not participate in meiosis. Uncertain that it really was a chromosome, he called it the "X element." After it was determined to actually be a chromosome, it became known as the "X chromosome."

The Y chromosome was identified as a sex-determining chromosome in 1905 by Nettie Stevens at Bryn Mawr College and separately by Edmund Beecher Wilson in unrelated studies. Nettie Stevens believed that sex was determined by the presence or absence of the Y chromosome, and that it paired with the X. She called it the "Y" chromosome simply following Henking's "X" with the next letter in the alphabet (Wikipedia, "Y chromosome," January 29, 2020).

Further: "All chromosomes normally appear as an amorphous blob under the microscope and only take on a well-defined shape during mitosis. This shape is vaguely X-shaped for all chromosomes. It is entirely coincidental that the Y chromosome, during mitosis, has two very short branches which can look merged under the microscope and appear as the descender of a Y-shape."

Creation of eggs and sperm

You may be wondering if you wind up with entire chromosomes identical to those of either parent. No, you don't (though a male child may inherit all or most of his father's Y chromosome, explained later with the *SRY* gene). Why not? Largely due to what's called crossing over (recombination) of paired chromosomes during formation of eggs and sperm in a process called meiosis. (The box following this section provides a high-level explanation of how crossing over works; it's not critical to the gist of the book, if you want to stick with the basics. But it's a fun read, and you may learn something new.)

Egg creation begins in the fetus, halts, and continues at puberty with monthly releases of a few newly completed eggs. Sperm creation in the male is continuous after puberty, with millions produced per day, each taking about two and a half months to mature.

When a sperm fertilizes an egg, the single set of 23 chromosomes in the egg plus the single set of 23 chromosomes in the sperm will restore pairings totaling 46 chromosomes in the zygote that will develop into the child.

What your biology teacher may or may not have taught you is that the usual process doesn't always progress smoothly. Offspring can wind up with just one sex chromosome (XO), or with three (XXX, XXY, XYY), or more (XXXX, XXYY, etc). We'll discuss these scenarios later.

Crossing over

How does crossing over, or recombination, work?

We talked about pairs of chromosomes. The two chromosomes of a pair are called homologous chromosomes, or homologues. We'll run through an example that could use any of the 22 autosomes, but we'll use chromosome 8. (X and Y crossover is a somewhat different story that we'll discuss later with the *SRY* gene.)

Let's say eggs are being created in Martha's body, and we'll pick chromosome 8 as an example. Martha has a chromosome 8 she inherited from her mother (we'll call this 8A) and another chromosome 8 that she inherited from her father (let's call this 8B). In the process of meiosis (specifically, during prophase I) that occurs when producing the egg and sperm cells, the chromosome homologues align in their pairs and cross over each other, with the members of each pair swapping portions of their chromosomes.

Normally, analogous portions are swapped, and the switching results in different versions of the same genes (alleles) on each chromosome. Occasionally, crossing over is unequal, causing gene deletion(s) on one chromosome and insertion(s) on the other. This can cause genetic disease or failure to develop (Speer, 2020).

During this crossing over process, swapping is likely to occur more frequently in the portions of each arm that are further from the centromere (the point of attachment of the two arms of a single chromosome).

Each pair of homologues undergoes multiple cross-over events. How many? Encyclopedia.com reports about 75 in females and 55 in males (Speer, 2020.)

In the example of Martha's eggs, chromosome 8A will swap some of its sections with chromosome 8B. The same process occurs when creating sperm in the male.

During subsequent phases of meiosis, random orientation of homologue pairs during cell division ensures further unique combinations of DNA. The combination of crossing over and random orientation of homologue pairs creates millions of possible gene combinations.

This process ultimately will create four eggs in Martha's example, each with one copy of chromosome 8 containing a unique mix of genes from 8A and 8B. Thus, each of the 23 chromosomes in the egg is a single homologue (no longer paired) having portions of DNA from Martha's mother and portions of DNA from Martha's father, with each egg being unique in its DNA content.

Similarly, in creation of sperm, the DNA content of each autosome will be unique. What's different about meiosis in sperm creation is that the two sex chromosomes are structured differently such that only about 5% of the Y chromosome has analogous genes on the X chromosome. Those portions, called the pseudoautosomal region (PAR) on each, do match up and *may* experience some crossing over. The rest of the Y chromosome undergoes some crossover with a palindrome copy of itself. (A palindrome looks or reads the same from either direction, as in "MOM" for example.) Under usual circumstances of meiosis, the Y chromosome inherited by a son will be either all or mostly a replica of the father's.

X chromosome inactivation

A note about the two X sex chromosomes in females: In some mammals, if both X chromosomes remained active in cells throughout the body, females could, "produce too many copies of proteins coded by X-linked genes," (LeVay, 2011, p. 174). To prevent this situation, during development of the female fetus one of the two X chromosomes present throughout the cells of the body is largely inactivated in each cell. The inactivated X chromosome is compacted into what is known as a Barr body (Ahn and Lee, 2008).

The "some mammals" group (including humans) that use the method of X inactivation briefly described here are the **eutherian mammals** – those that have a placenta. The mammalian classifications that this does not include are the marsupials (e.g., kangaroo and opossum) and the monotremes (e.g., platypus and echidna). For simplicity, this discussion is limited to the eutherian mammals.

To learn more, including the actual implementation of inactivation, you might start with an article by Janice Y. Ahn and J. T. Lee of Harvard Medical School: "X Chromosome: X Inactivation" published in 2008 by Nature Education. As of this writing, it is available on the nature.com website here: https://www.nature.com/scitable/topicpage/x-chromosome-x-inactivation-323/

It must be noted that not all of the genes of the inactivated chromosome are actually inactivated, those remaining active being dubbed "escape genes." These escape genes make up about 15% of the X chromosome's genes in humans, and may be implicated in sex-linked traits (Berletch et al., 2011).

Normally, each of the two X chromosomes undergoes inactivation in about half the cells of the body. This allows about a 50 - 50 ratio for expression of the maternal and the paternal X chromosomes. However, at times the inactivation has been found to be skewed toward one X or the other.

Extreme X-inactivation skewing appears to be higher in mothers of male homosexuals. Normally at about 4% in the control group of the studies, the correlation was found to be 13% in mothers of gay men, and 23% in mothers having at least two gay sons. According to a report published by PubMed, these findings support, "a role for the X chromosome in regulating sexual orientation in a subgroup of gay men," (Bocklandt et al., 2005).

A familiar example of the scattered expression and inactivation of the two X chromosomes is the calico or tortoiseshell cat. The fur pigmentation gene is X-linked, and depending on which X chromosome is inactivated and which is expressed, the fur in that area will be either black or orange (Ahn and Lee, 2008). This explains why – and a bit of how – tortoiseshell and calico cats are almost always female. Meet Mimi (pictured below), a tortoiseshell who's sitting by my knee as I write. Mimi's color distribution is fairly even. Her friend Kayla is nearly all black, and Kylie is nearly all orange (neither pictured here).

What happens with inactivation when an individual has more than two X chromosomes? (We've mentioned that more than two sex chromosomes can occur; there is more discussion of these cases later.) In their article "X Chromosome: X Inactivation" (2008), Ahn and Lee show that the inactivating factor (*XIST* RNA, for those who want to look it up) appears to be present in amounts that correlate to the number of "extra" X chromosomes. In XO Turner syndrome females, the single X chromosome remains active; there is no second X present to be inactivated. In an XY male, there is no second X, and no inactivation. An XXY Klinefelter syndrome male would experience inactivation of the second X in a manner similar to an XX female.

In the cases mentioned previously in which the cells contain more than two X chromosomes - XXX females, XXXY males, and those with yet higher numbers of X chromosomes, higher amounts of *XIST* RNA are present than when only the second X needs to be inactivated. These genetic conditions are discussed in the chapter Complexities of Genetic Sex.

Brain differentiation

The other aspect of gender determination that you may or may not have learned in biology class is twofold:

1. Certain structures within the brain become differentiated to varying degrees as male or female in the womb.
2. Genes and hormones play a role in this differentiation of male and female brain development.

In her studies of brain differences between women and men, Anne Moir (*Brain Sex: The Real Difference Between Men and Women*, Anne Moir and David Jessel, Lyle Stuart, 1992) concludes that male and female brains develop differently in the human fetus, and that the default form is a female brain. That is, regardless of the sex chromosomes of the fetus, with no exposure to male or female hormones, the brain and reproductive organs would develop in the female pattern. (Supporting evidence lies in cases involving the *SRY* gene, described in our Complexities of Genetic Sex chapter.)

Dick Swaab confirms that as of this writing in 2019, it still appears that absent male hormones, the default brain development proceeds in the female pattern. Following the mosaic concept, we must keep in mind that this differentiation is in the context of the specific structures that develop on the female-male continuum rather than the brain as a whole.

Several weeks into embryonic development, a gene (or genes) on the Y chromosome kick-start a deviation from the default female development of the fetus, causing certain brain structures to develop in the male pattern, and the body to develop male reproductive organs and genitalia. We'll talk about how this process can go awry in the Complexities of Genetic Sex chapter.

Development of a male brain results from embryonic exposure to androgens (male hormones) beginning at around six weeks' development. The amount and timing of male hormones determine the structures affected in the brain, and the degree to which those structures become male. Development of male reproductive organs and genitalia are similarly influenced. Moir and Jessel cite page after page of research papers and other sources from which their conclusions are drawn. Multiple studies and research from respected institutions confirm these findings.

A journey of many paths

Along the developmental route from conception to sexual definition in both brain and sex organs, there is a fascinating array of primary and alternate paths that can be taken. In addition to the more familiar XX female and XY male, each standardly equipped, there may be cases of genetic female XX developing male genitalia or genetic male XY developing female sex organs, or any combination in between. More on this, later.

The developmental and functional differences between male and female brains is assumed here. It is not the purpose of this book to present convincing material in that regard. Likewise, I am not here to convince the reader of the hormonal effects on fetal brain and sex organ development. That, too, is accepted as fact. (You could spend days, weeks, or longer reading scientific publications on this.)

We will, however, discuss a brief summary of the different presentations and behaviors of the male versus female brain. Then, we'll look at various routes that biology can take in the process of determining both brain and anatomical presentation of sex.

The Road Not Taken
-Robert Frost

Two roads diverged in a yellow wood,
And sorry I could not travel both
And be one traveler, long I stood
And looked down one as far as I could
To where it bent in the undergrowth;

Then took the other, as just as fair,
And having perhaps the better claim,
Because it was grassy and wanted wear;
Though as for that the passing there
Had worn them really about the same,

And both that morning equally lay
In leaves no step had trodden black.
Oh, I kept the first for another day!
Yet knowing how way leads on to way,
I doubted if I should ever come back.

I shall be telling this with a sigh
Somewhere ages and ages hence:
Two roads diverged in a wood, and I—
I took the one less traveled by,
And that has made all the difference.

A Moment of Reflection

Let's take a moment to relax and reflect. Think about your childhood days. Playing outdoors, enjoying the natural world. Relationships with parents, relatives, friends. Experiencing life. Exploring. Growing up. Your experiences of others and of yourself. How do you feel, yourself, as you go through life?

When I was a child, I felt insulted when my cousin, Dennis, called me a tomboy. Was it because we were playing with friction cars together on our grandparents' dining room floor that he called me that? Right then, I had more interest in the physics, the feel, and the experience of friction cars than in something inert like a doll – though I had my doll phases, too.

This example of gender contrast – preference for wheeled vehicles versus dolls as a child's play toys – is not based in sociology or effects of society or culture, but has been confirmed by multiple studies to be "built in." Even juvenile male rhesus monkeys prefer wheeled vehicles (Hassett et al., 2008). Separate studies with vervet monkeys (Alexander and Hines, 2002) produced similar findings, and additionally verified that female vervets preferred plush toys.

It has been remarkable to me that even my young bulls come to examine my car when I drive out into the field, while the cows ignore it and keep grazing.

When married, it was common for me to be outside putting up fence around the pasture while my husband was in the kitchen fixing dinner. Yet, we also had periods of time during which I enjoyed shopping and cooking dinner while he was out making a living running a backhoe or 'dozer.

There's flexibility in these scenarios. There probably is in your life, too. Think about the fluctuations in your experiences. There are times you follow traditionally women's pursuits, and at other times, men's. It makes sense. Swapping chores and cooking with your partner allows you both to do whichever you prefer in that moment. Adaptability and variation have allowed the human race to survive and thrive over many thousands of years.

We all embrace both female and male behaviors and tasks, and perhaps at times exhibit strengths normally attributed to the other sex. Yet, most of us identify strongly and definitively as one gender or the other – as man or woman.

Keep in mind that women produce small amounts of male hormones along with larger amounts of female hormones, and men produce small amounts of female hormones in addition to larger amounts of male hormones. It's natural that these "opposite sex" hormones have a minor impact on our bodies and brains.

The point is that in each of us, there is not a complete and total divide. None of us expresses only male or only female characteristics and pursues only men's or only women's traditional roles and behaviors. Each of us is a bit of a mix – what the scientific research community calls a mosaic. I think we enjoy that freedom.

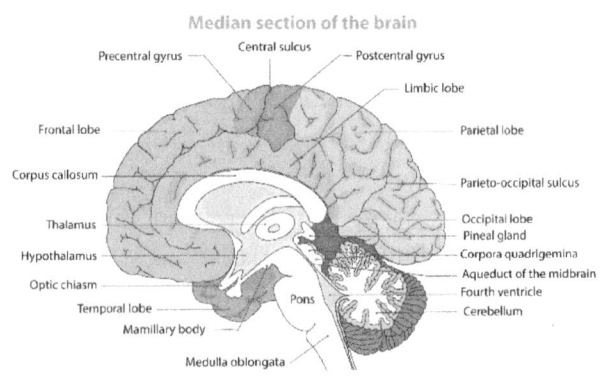

Median section of the brain

The Brain: Male vs. Female

In the context of sexual differentiation, brains develop along a continuum between female and male. We'll begin with an oversimplification by talking about the endpoints of the continuum: female and male. Later, we'll advance to the actual mosaic blend of both.

Sexual differentiation

Some areas of the human brain are sexually differentiated – there are anatomical and functional differences between a male brain and a female brain. In general, the brain structures that differ in size and function between the male and female brain possess more sex hormone receptors than do other areas of the brain.

The male brain is generally larger than the female brain, which is consistent with the male body being larger (taller and heavier) than the female body. There are some women who are taller and more heavily built than some men, but the average man will be taller and heavier than the average woman. We're speaking in general terms of averages. In our discussion of the few brain structures known to differ between men and women, keep in mind that differences in brain structure and function, likewise, are generalizations with some overlap.

Hypothalamus

Early studies searching for physical brain differences between male and female go back at least to the 1970s, if not earlier, and focused on the hypothalamus – the structure that controls sexual behavior. Functions that the hypothalamus regulates, in addition to sexual behavior, are: appetite, body temperature, biological rhythms, sleep, and short-term memory. Additionally, the hypothalamus works with the pituitary gland to regulate hormone levels.

Several areas within the hypothalamus have been confirmed to exhibit both structural and functional differences between males and females. Studies have shown that whether female- or male-patterned, these characteristics do not change if the adult brain is exposed to opposite-sex hormones. This result is consistent with studies reported by Moir and Jessel, among others.

Hippocampus

The hippocampus is a central portion of the brain used in memory and learning. As a percentage of total brain size, a female hippocampus is larger and both structurally and functionally different than a male hippocampus.

Amygdala

The amygdala is a small structure found in each brain hemisphere (one on the right side of the brain; another on the left side of the brain), and is involved in experiencing and recalling emotions. These are larger in the male brain, and function differently than in the female brain. Events triggering strong negative emotions in women are associated with activity in the left amygdala; in men they are associated with activity in the right amygdala.

Corpus callosum

The corpus callosum is a structure that connects the two brain hemispheres, and is larger in the female brain. This is consistent with the female brain communicating and coordinating more activity between the two hemispheres than does the male brain.

Cerebral cortex

The cerebral cortex is a rind-like structure that overlays both hemispheres of the brain. In males, the cerebral cortex is thicker on the right side; in females, it is thicker on the left.

Experiments have demonstrated that the degree of male hormone exposure during the fetal stage of development determines male versus female patterning.

***

Let's look briefly at the strengths of the male-patterned brain and the female-patterned brain. These are areas in which multiple tests and studies have shown either males or females to repeatedly excel over the other, with multiple sources reporting consistent results.

Male strengths

- Spatial ability – the ability to accurately visualize, rotate, place, and otherwise mentally manipulate three-dimensional objects and abstract spatial relationships
- Mathematical ability – consistently demonstrated superior math skills

- Hand-eye coordination, such as that exercised in baseball, tennis, or golf

Men are more things-oriented than people-oriented. They are more likely than women to suffer from alcoholism, drug addiction, dyslexia, autism, or schizophrenia.

Female strengths

- Communication – grammar, spelling, reading comprehension, writing ability, verbal communication, language fluency
- Auditory acuity
- Sensitivity to visual, auditory, and other behavioral cues

Women are more people-oriented than things-oriented. They are more likely than men to experience PTSD (post-traumatic stress disorder) or clinical depression.

Men and women also differ in their fields of vision, sense of taste, sense of smell, and memory.

These differences in aptitudes and sensitivities are based on structural and functional differences in the brain. That is, they have a biological basis.

Sexual Differentiation and the Fetal Brain

Human sexual differentiation occurs through multiple stages of fetal development.

1. Initial post-fertilization development of the embryo appears undifferentiated in terms of sex.
2. Sex organs develop during weeks six to twelve, although internal and external sex organs may not form concurrently.
3. During the second half of pregnancy, portions of the brain differentiate along male or female lines, with different structures developing at different times, generally independently of one another.

Each type of differentiation depends on the degree to which the fetus produces (or doesn't produce) male hormones. Sexual differentiation additionally may be influenced by drugs, environmental chemicals, or other factors that mimic or suppress female or male hormones. We'll get into more detail about these factors and their effects in later chapters.

At about six weeks, under usual circumstances, an XX female embryo will continue to develop along physical female lines. An XY male embryo will develop cells that produce male hormones (testosterone and other androgens). These hormones trigger development of male genitalia and testes. In sufficient amounts at specific times, male hormones will trigger development of the brain into the male pattern.

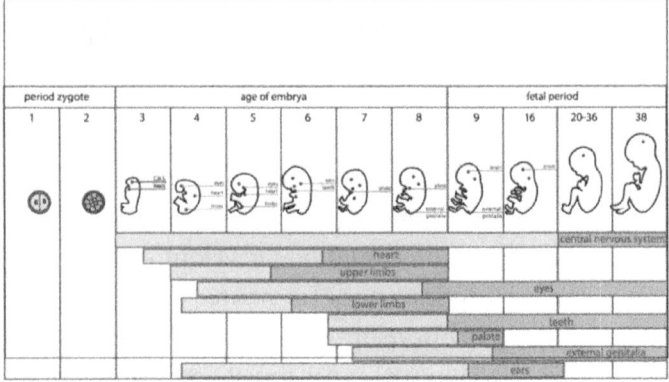

period zygote		age of embryo						fetal period			
1	2	3	4	5	6	7	8	9	16	20-36	38

central nervous system

heart

upper limbs

lower limbs

eyes

teeth

palate

external genitalia

ears

The timing and degree to which the embryo is exposed to male hormones determine the degree to which the fetus will develop male characteristics. Specific timing and degree of hormonal exposure can render differing results in the anatomy of internal and external sex organs and the patterning and function of specific brain structures.

In *We Are Our Brains: From the Womb to Alzheimer's*, Dick Swaab tells us that brain cells are created very rapidly in the womb and shortly after birth, then more slowly until about the age of four. The brain's process of maturing lasts much longer, with maturation of the prefrontal cortex occurring at age twenty-five. "Every facet of brain cell development can be disrupted by chemical substances during pregnancy," (Swaab, *We Are Our Brains*, p. 45). The point at which these effects become evident can range from birth until much later, with reproductive issues potentially becoming evident only in adulthood.

Certain brain structures may "overproduce" cells and synapses during fetal development, later pruning back those that are weaker and less active. Some of these structures are associated with degrees of maleness or femaleness, which we'll discuss later.

During the period of fetal differentiation, one's gender identity (feeling of being a man or a woman) is set in the brain. It will remain set, regardless of future exposure to sex hormones. Let's look at this in more detail.

Absent exposure to male hormones (or being insensitive to testosterone, as in androgen insensitivity syndrome (AIS), an XY genetically male fetus can develop physically as a female, and appear to be a girl, with female genitalia, at birth.

Similarly, if a genetically female XX embryo is exposed to male hormones (or chemicals that mimic male hormones) at this time, the fetus can develop physical male characteristics and genitalia, and at birth appear to be a boy. Such exposure may occur as a result of medical treatment of the mother during pregnancy.

With less-pronounced variance in exposure to male hormones, physical development of sexually-differentiating organs and brain structures may be less marked. Sex organs may be incompletely or ambiguously developed. A baby may be born with partial or full sets of both male and female reproductive apparatus. Male-female patterning of specific brain structures may be ambiguous.

It is only during embryonic and fetal development that the brain exhibits such plasticity based on exposure to (or absence of) male hormones. An adult male-patterned brain (whether in a female XX or a male XY body) exposed to female hormones will not physically restructure itself into a female brain pattern. Likewise, an adult female-patterned brain (in either a female XX or a male XY body) exposed to male hormones will not restructure itself into a male brain pattern.

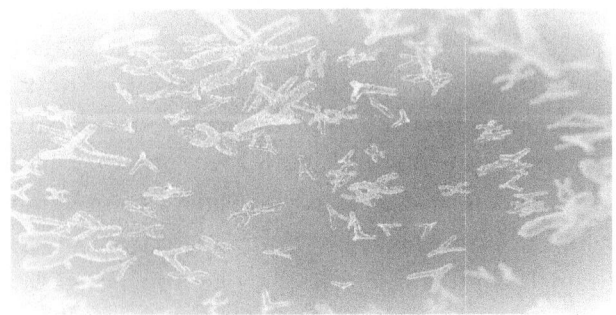

Chromosome image © Adobe Stock / rost9

Complexities of Genetic Sex

In biology class, we all learned that girls are born with two X sex chromosomes (XX) and that boys are born with an X and a Y sex chromosome (XY). This is the simple binary sex that we readily understand, and most of us haven't been taught the complexities beyond those two simple configurations.

Genetic sexual determination based on configuration of sex chromosomes is not simply binary. What the complexity boils down to is that presence of a Y chromosome, regardless of the number of X chromosomes present, defines a genetic male; absence of a Y chromosome defines a genetic female. Sexual anatomy is not so simply defined, nor even determined.

Following is a list of some known combinations of sex chromosomes that occur naturally. Conditions potentially associated with alternate sex chromosome configurations are milder than conditions associated with non-sex (the other 22 pair) chromosome anomalies and may go unnoticed until puberty.

XX
Usual female configuration.

XY
Usual male configuration.

XXX – Trisomy X

Variously known as triple X syndrome; XXX syndrome; 47 XXX; trisomy X; triplo X. A female individual with an extra X chromosome in each of her body's cells, usually inherited from the mother (more frequently older mothers). Affects about 1 in 1,000 females. She may be taller than average but otherwise is not likely to exhibit unusual physical characteristics.

The online *Merck Manual, Consumer Version* states that rare cases of infants with four or five X chromosomes have been identified; likelihood of potential symptoms increases with the number of extra X chromosomes.

XXY – Klinefelter syndrome

Genetic condition in which a male individual carries multiple X sex chromosomes along with a Y. Occurs in about 1 of 500 male births, many of which may go undiagnosed. More than two X chromosomes may occur, such as XXXXXY. The Association for X and Y Chromosome Variations (AXYS) at genetic.org reports that some subtle physical symptoms may exist, such as: slightly taller stature; small chest depression; flat feet; curved little finger (clinodactyly); low muscle tone (hypotonia); undescended or small testes; radioulnar synostosis, which can cause difficulty in straightening the elbow or rotating the forearm (AXYS, 2016; NIH, 2017). *Merck Manuals* reports that most are tall with long arms and legs; may have wider hips, sparse facial hair, enlarged breasts; or be prone to diabetes mellitus, lung disease, hypothyroidism, or breast cancer (Merck Manuals Consumer Version, 2018). They usually are infertile. This condition may go unnoticed until puberty, though it may cause difficulties with speech, reading, planning, or language (Merck Manuals Consumer Version, 2018). Symptom severity tends to increase with the number of additional X chromosomes.

XO – Turner syndrome

Variously known as Turner's syndrome, XO syndrome, Monosomy X. Most XO fetuses spontaneously abort. Those who survive may present a number of associated symptoms and are generally infertile.

XYY – Jacobs syndrome

Also known as 47,XYY syndrome. Occurs in about 1 of 1,000 male births. May exhibit learning disabilities, attention deficit, or hyperactivity.

As a practical matter, I suggest that anyone affected directly or indirectly by these aneuploidy conditions (XXX, XXY, XYY and related) may find information and support at the genetic.org website and download its documents and guides, including *Living with Klinefelter Syndrome (47,XXY), Trisomy X (47,XXX), or 47,XYY*: https://genetic.org/wp-content/uploads/2016/08/LivingWithKlinefelterSy ndromeTrisomyX47XYY.pdf. The author describes her guide as follows (p.6):

> The guide is not a research article, but rather provides information for affected individuals, their family members, and the professionals who work with them. It emphasizes the range of functioning and of symptoms that characterize the SCA

conditions of 47,XXY; 47,XYY; 47,XXX, and variations of these disorders.

I do provide the bibliography of scientific articles that I used to summarize functioning and best practices, but the text is not footnoted in the way that a peer-reviewed article would be. While previous brief summaries have shied away from discussing the more controversial areas, such as overlap with autism spectrum disorders and concern that some XXY adults express about gender identity and sexual preference, this guide discusses what people have told me. It is not a scientific paper. My goal is to provide readable and accurate information, and to help families see their loved ones in the context of what others have experienced.

At 204 pages, this guide provides a vast wealth of information covering a broad range of topics relevant to these conditions. It begins with covering amniocentesis testing showing these conditions are present (and how doctors and parents respond), as well as a brief explanation of how they can occur during mitosis (cell division) early in the development of the embryo. The guide includes statistics, very inclusive information on living with and handling symptoms, and is partially based on input from over 800 survey respondents, as well as scientific research. The document is provided at the time of this writing on the AXYS website, at no cost.

SRY gene

The *SRY* gene (sex-determining region of the Y chromosome) is crucial for normal development of male reproductive organs, and is located on the short arm of the

Y chromosome at Yp11.2 (Y chromosome, short arm (p), region 1, band 1, sub-band 2). The *SRY* gene produces a protein that binds to specific regions of DNA to affect the activity of specific other genes. This kickstarts development of testes and suppresses development of female internal reproductive organs (NCBI, "SRY Gene," 2020).

Though the X and Y chromosomes are very different from one another, they share a short similar region (the pseudoautosomal region, or PAR) at the end of their short arms. This PAR comprises about 5% of the Y chromosome. In Encyclopedia.com, Speer reports that normally no crossing over occurs involving the Y chromosome during meiosis, and a son inherits a Y chromosome that is a duplicate of his father's. However, Speer describes how the pseudoautosomal regions of the X and Y chromosomes *may* go through a crossover process during meiosis in a manner similar to the process for the 22 autosomes.

The *SRY* gene is located near the pseudoautosomal region on the Y chromosome. As explained in the crossing over section, normally only analogous areas (alleles) are swapped between the two homologues of a pair, though on occasion the swap is uneven. In crossing over involving the X and Y chromosomes, normally only the pseudoautosomal region is involved.

However, it is possible for the swapped region to extend beyond the pseudoautosomal region and include the *SRY* gene. In this rare instance, the Y chromosome loses its *SRY* gene to the X chromosome.

If a sperm carrying the Y chromosome that has lost the *SRY* gene fertilizes an egg (X), this can result in a genetic XY male developing physically as a female.

If a sperm carrying the X chromosome that has gained the *SRY* gene fertilizes an egg (X), the resulting genetic XX female can develop to all appearances as a male (Speer, 2020).

It is difficult to nail down if, when, or how often PAR recombination *actually* occurs between the X and Y chromosomes. Evidently it does occur (and may overstep its intended boundary) due to the fact that the *SRY* gene has been found translocated from the Y to the X chromosome.

The non-PAR portion of the Y chromosome undergoes a version of crossing over with a palindrome copy of itself, which is beneficial in correcting errors in the genes. ("MOM" is an example of a palindrome – it looks the same from either direction.)

If the crossing over between the X and Y PARs does occur, a son would inherit *most* of the DNA from his father's Y chromosome since the PAR is such a small portion (5%). In cases it does not occur, a son would inherit a duplicate of his father's Y chromosome (assuming no errors occur during meiosis).

Swyer syndrome

This is a condition in which genetic males (XY) develop with female sex characteristics – typical external genitalia, uterus, fallopian tubes, but with undeveloped "streak" gonads rather than functioning ovaries or testes.

People with Swyer syndrome usually identify as female and are raised as girls. Lacking ovaries, they do not produce eggs, but may be able to give birth with donated eggs or embryos.

SRY gene (discussed above) mutations account for about 15% of cases. *MAP3K1* gene mutations account for up to another 18%. This gene affects development of sexual characteristics in the womb, decreasing male and increasing female differentiation. *DHH, NR5A1,* and other gene mutations, as well as hormones administered to the mother while pregnant account for another small number of cases, while causes for the majority remain unidentified. This condition is also known as "gonadal dysgenesis, 46,XY" and additional similar names, and occurs in about 1 in 80,000 people. (National Institutes of Health, "Swyer Syndrome," 2020).

46,XX testicular disorder

In about 80% of cases, this condition results from the scenario described above, in which crossover during meiosis occurs between the X and Y chromosomes beyond their pseudoautosomal regions, resulting in the

SRY gene from the Y chromosome crossing over to the X chromosome during sperm development in the father. When this is the cause, it is known as *SRY*-positive 46,XX testicular disorder of sex development. In this case, a genetic female (XX) presents with male sexual characteristics usually including male genitalia.

In the other 20% of cases, either a genetic cause has not been identified, or has been associated with other genes (*SOX3*, *SOX9*, discussed in Appendix A). These cases are known as *SRY*-negative 46,XX testicular disorder of sex development, and are more likely to present with ambiguous genitalia.

In general, testes may be small or undescended. The urethra opening may be located on the underside of the penis, a condition known as hypospadias. Most identify as male and are raised as male, but usually are infertile. They may require hormone treatment upon reaching puberty to develop male characteristics such as facial hair and deeper voice, and to prevent breast development. They may be shorter than the average male. This condition occurs in about 1 in 20,000 people who present with a male appearance (Genetics Home Reference. "46,XX testicular disorder," 2020).

***

This may not be an exhaustive list of potential sex chromosome combinations or genetic impacts on sexual development. However, it does serve to demonstrate that human sex is a complex matter rather than a strictly binary configuration.

Effects of Fetal Hormones on Expression of Genetic Sex

We have just listed several possible combinations of sex chromosomes in humans. Physical expression of those genetic combinations can be altered by embryonic exposure or lack of exposure to androgens, i.e., male hormones.

Extensive studies have determined that an embryo's degree of exposure to male hormones beginning at about six weeks' development will determine the degree of maleness and/or femaleness in patterning of the brain. Lacking such exposure as an embryo, a human brain will, by default, develop with the female pattern. Even a genetically male XY embryo would develop a female-patterned brain if it weren't exposed to male hormones.

weeks

| 1 | 2 | 3 | 4 | 5 | 6 | 7 | 8 | 9 | 16 | 20-36 | 38 |

A genetically male embryo will begin to differentiate structures to produce male hormones – androgens including testosterone – about six weeks into its development. The presence of these hormones will initiate development of male reproductive organs as well as the male patterning of certain structures within the brain.

Normally not producing significant quantities of male hormones, a genetically female embryo will develop female reproductive organs and predominantly female patterning of the brain.

That said, magnetic resonance imaging (MRI) to study comparative volumes of the known sexually differentiated regions of the brain (in which male pattern and female pattern differ in volume) has shown that a brain with all of these regions demonstrating the male pattern, or all demonstrating the female pattern are rare (Joel et al., 2015). The vast majority of us possess a mosaic of structures, some of which lean toward the male and others toward the female pattern (Joel, Garcia-Falgueras, and Swaab 2019, pp. 2 - 5).

Male-patterned brains develop to the extent that they are exposed to male hormones (or certain look-alike chemicals) during their embryonic state. Healthy functioning of hormone receptors in each of the affected structures plays an important role in ensuring sufficient association to initiate male patterning. Each of these structures is uniquely affected, and each likely develops at a different time. Consequently, fluctuating concentrations of male hormones can cause different sex-related brain structures to develop with male patterning to differing degrees. Brain structures affecting gender identity and sexual orientation develop at different times, so may be either congruent or incongruent with one another.

Considerable study has gone into discovering how the timing of exposure to higher or lower levels of sex hormones can affect which particular brain structures, and to what degree. German scientist Gunter Dörner and American scientist Milton Diamond each independently have proposed that the development of maleness or femaleness of the brain occurs in stages.

Dörner proposed three brain centers that develop (1) an individual's sex organs, (2) sex/mating preference, and (3) gender identity. The first of these guides the development of male or female physical characteristics. The second occurs in the hypothalamus, which directs adult sexual and mating behavior. The third determines patterns of female versus male behavior, such as being passive versus aggressive; timid or adventurous; and degree of social behavior and expression. These patterns of behavior become more strongly expressed at puberty due to the increase in sex hormones.

Dr. Diamond proposed four stages rather than three, which occur roughly in reverse order from Dörner's. First, sexual behavior patterning. Second, sexual or gender identity. Third, sexual object choice, or mating preference. Fourth, control center for the physical development of sexual organs.

Dick Swaab tells us from more recent research that male – female anatomy develops in the first half of pregnancy, while sex-specific differentiation in brain structures occurs during the second.

Fluctuations in hormone levels across these phases of male versus female development can result in an individual presentation that is neither consistently male nor consistently female, but rather more male in one or more areas and more female in others.

The time for developing male versus female brain patterning is limited to the period of development in the womb. Exposure to female hormones will not change an adult male-patterned brain into a female-patterned brain; male hormones will not change an adult female-patterned brain into a male-patterned one. Adult exposure to hormones may change certain characteristics of the body (e.g., breast development, hair growth) or behaviors such as degree of aggression versus passivity.

Hypothalamus revisited

Several areas within the hypothalamus have been confirmed to have both structural and functional differences between human males and females.

The interstitial nucleus of the anterior hypothalamus, subdivision 1, (INAH-1), also known as the intermediate nucleus or sexually dimorphic nucleus of the preoptic area, is one structure studied. At birth, human females and males both have about the same number of INAH-1 cells. This number increases after birth in both, reaching its maximum at two to four years of age. The cell numbers begin to decrease in women around puberty, and in men at around age fifty. The cell number in adult women is measurably lower than that in adult men (Joel, Garcia-Falgueras, and Swaab 2019, pp. 5 - 6).

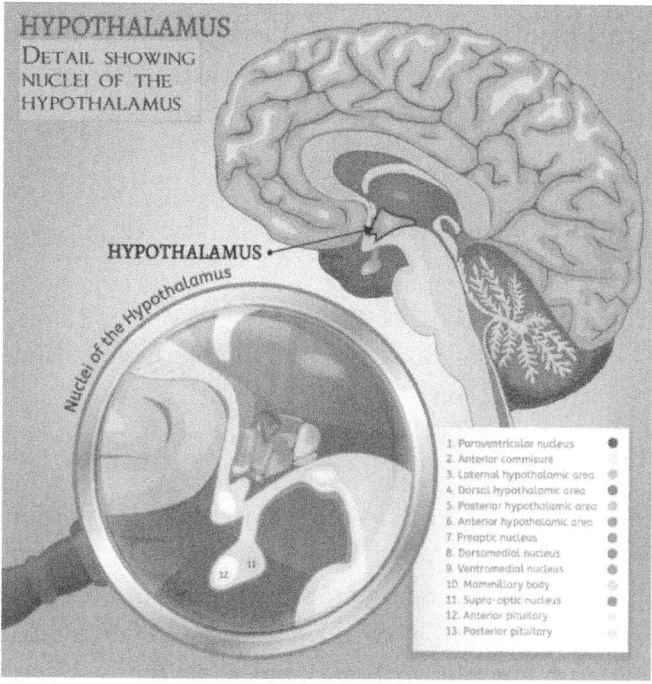

Hypothalamus © Adobe Stock / Double Brain

In the INAH-3 (interstitial nucleus of the anterior hypothalamus, subdivision 3, a subnucleus of the uncinate nucleus), cell numbers are higher in women than in men. It appears that in women, the same factor may affect both the INAH-1 and INAH-3 differences, though in opposite directions, with the INAH-3 larger and the INAH-1 smaller than that of men. In general, however, it appears that sexually dimorphic regions develop their female or male patterning independently of one another (Joel, Garcia-Falgueras, and Swaab 2019, pp. 2 - 5).

Hypothalamus and sexual orientation

As of original publication (2019) and subsequent updates (up to June 2022), three specific sexually-differentiated brain structures have been associated with sexual orientation.

Sites within the hypothalamus implicated in sexual orientation:

- suprachiasmatic nucleus (SCN)
- interstitial nucleus of the anterior hypothalamus subdivision 3 (INAH-3)
- anterior commissure

Suprachiasmatic nuclei exist in the right and left portions of the hypothalamus. They function as the master biological clock, sending messages to entrain the body's peripheral clocks, thus synchronizing the body's circadian rhythms. The human body's innate rhythm is slightly longer than 24 hours, with estimates ranging from 24 hours 11 minutes (plus or minus 16 minutes, as determined by a study by Czeisler et al. at Harvard) to 24.3 hours (24 hours 18 minutes, as reported by LENScience, published by the Liggins Institute at The University of Auckland, New Zealand); evidently, it's difficult to determine precisely. The SCN maintains accuracy daily via external stimuli such as ambient light detected by special ganglion cells in the eyes' retinas, and transmitted via optic nerves to each SCN, located above the optic chiasm. This is the method by which the 24-hour clock is maintained. (More information about the body's biological clock: https://thebrain.mcgill.ca/flash/i/i_11/i_11_cr/i_11_cr_hor/i_11_cr_hor.html).

The anterior commissure is a bundle of nerve fibers connecting the olfactory bulb and areas of the cerebrum between the left and right sides of the brain.

Dr. Swaab's research has shown that the INAH-3 is related to both sexual orientation and gender identity.

Hypothalamus, gender identity, and transsexuality

Evidence has been found to indicate a relationship between dimorphism in the human hypothalamus and gender identity. Cited in the research is a specific structure near the hypothalamus, the BSTc (central nucleus of the bed nucleus of the stria terminalis). The BSTc is about 40% larger in the male brain than in the female brain, and has nearly double the somatostatin neurons. This site has been associated with gender identity, but not with sexual orientation.

Dick Swaab reported in 1995 that correlations exist between human transsexuality and the BSTc. He further elaborates in *We Are Our Brains* that their study used postmortem donor brains, which explains both the twenty years necessary to acquire the study material and that there was just the one female-to-male transsexual subject.

It was found that genetically male, male-to-female transsexuals (reported to occur in 1 in 10,000 individuals) had a female-patterned BSTc.

Observations obtained from a single genetically female, female-to-male transsexual (occurring in 1 in 30,000 individuals) showed the BSTc was constructed in the male pattern, with larger size and number of somatostatin neurons.

Such evidence indicates that a mismatch between the genetic sex chromosomes (with congruent anatomy) and the pattern of the BSTc may cause feelings of being the right gender in the wrong body. These findings support the theory that in transsexuals, the first half of fetal development (in which sex organ differentiation occurs) and the second half of fetal development (in which male-female brain differentiation occurs) were subject to inconsistent exposure to sex hormones.

Dick Swaab's 1995 findings were supported in 2008 by Ivanka Savic's studies using functional brain scans of living male-to-female transsexuals who had not yet taken hormones or undergone surgery.

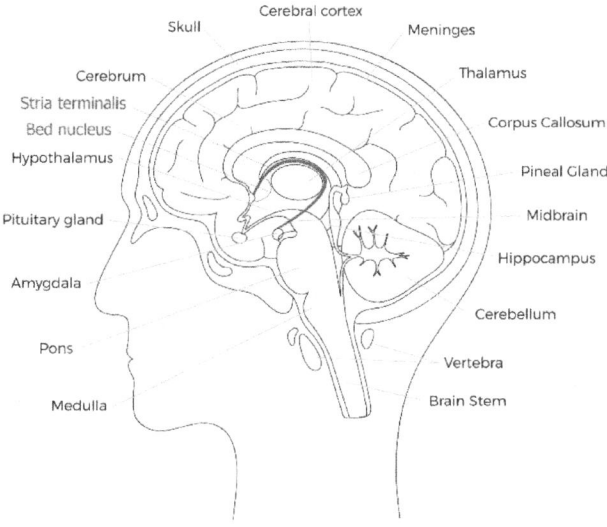

The BSTc is not the sole structure associated with an individual's gender identity; also associated are the infundibulum nucleus and the interstitial nucleus of the anterior hypothalamus, subdivision 3 (INAH-3), in short:

- Central nucleus of the bed nucleus of the stria terminalis (BSTc)
- Infundibulum nucleus
- Interstitial nucleus of the anterior hypothalamus, subdivision 3 (INAH-3)

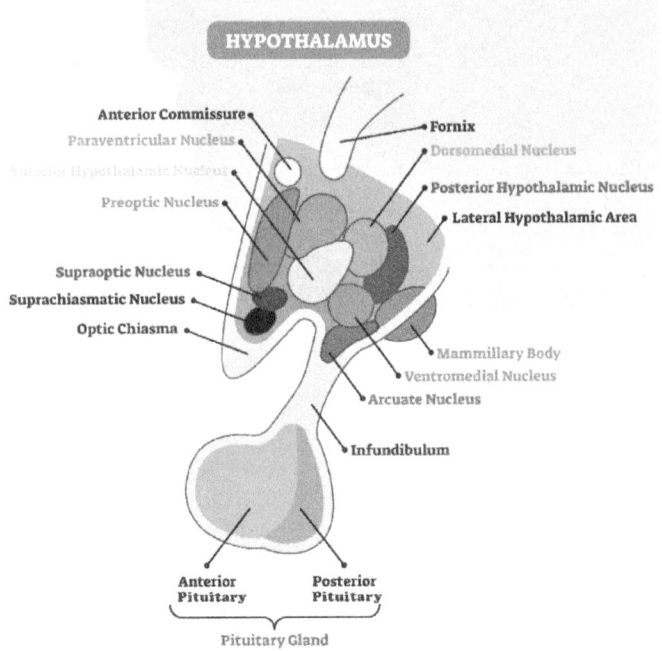

HYPOTHALAMUS

Anterior Commissure
Paraventricular Nucleus
Anterior Hypothalamic Nucleus
Preoptic Nucleus

Fornix
Dorsomedial Nucleus
Posterior Hypothalamic Nucleus
Lateral Hypothalamic Area

Supraoptic Nucleus
Suprachiasmatic Nucleus
Optic Chiasma

Mammillary Body
Ventromedial Nucleus
Arcuate Nucleus

Infundibulum

Anterior Pituitary   Posterior Pituitary

Pituitary Gland

Additional structures yet to be identified, both within the hypothalamus and elsewhere in the brain, may influence gender identity and/or sexual orientation.

Body mapping

There is a condition called Body Integrity Identity Disorder (BIID) in which a person very strongly feels that a part of their body doesn't belong. These feelings are so strong that many will go to extreme measures to get the offending part (usually a lower left leg or lower left arm) removed. Dick Swaab gives a nice discussion of this condition in *We Are Our Brains* (pp. 52 – 54) and additional examples in *Our Creative Brains* (XXII.2).

Our inner body map is created in the brain during early development in the womb, though currently it is unknown how this process on occasion goes awry. In the case of an involved leg, brain scans show different responses in the frontal and parietal cortices between the accepted and rejected legs when touched.

Swaab points out that in both BIID and in transsexuality, the individual typically knows from an early age that their anatomy is at variance with how they feel. It's interesting that nineteen percent of BIID patients also have gender identity issues, and thirty-eight percent are homosexual or bisexual.

Swaab reports that in 2007, V.S. Ramachandran published a hypothesis and provisional findings that the neural body map of a male-to-female transsexual lacks a penis, and the neural body map of a female-to-male transsexual lacks breasts, as they were not mapped during brain development (Swaab, We Are Our Brains, p. 70). It would be interesting to confirm that such a correlation does, indeed, exist.

Genetics and hormones

Genetic female (XX) with typically female sex organs and female brain pattern, and genetic male (XY) with typically male sex organs and male brain pattern are the two binary development patterns with which we're all familiar. But there are more possibilities.

Genetic sex (the sex chromosomes) and male versus female brain pattern can contradict one another due to exposure or lack of exposure to hormones in the embryo.

Timing of exposure also is a factor. Sex organs develop during the first months of pregnancy. Sexual differentiation of the brain occurs during the second half of pregnancy. Therefore, these two processes can be influenced independently. Further, different regions of the brain develop at different times, and may follow varying degrees of hormone-dependent male versus female development.

Consider that in humans and certain other mammals the presence of a Y chromosome classifies the individual as a male; an individual possessing one or more X chromosomes with no Y is classified as a genetic female.

A genetically female embryo (XX, XO, XXX, etc.) that is exposed to male hormones *or to chemicals that mimic male hormones* during these critical phases of fetal development may develop wholly or partially male reproductive organs and a male-patterned brain.

A genetically male fetus (XY, XXYY, etc.) with absent or lower levels of androgens may develop wholly or partially female reproductive organs and a female-patterned brain. He may have sufficient amounts of androgens to initiate development of male sex organs, but insufficient quantity, later, to fully develop the brain into the male pattern. Due to the female brain patterning, he may feel like a female in a male body (transgender, transsexual).

To be clear, it's both the brain and the body that may develop with portions following the male pattern and other portions following the female pattern, regardless of genetic sex of the individual.

Depending on the dose and timing of hormone exposure, the fetus may develop consistently male, consistently female, or with a complete or incomplete combination of male and female reproductive organs. The brain may develop predominantly following the female pattern, the male pattern, or a mix of the two.

Adrenogenital Syndrome, or Congenital Adrenal Hyperplasia

There is a condition known as adrenogenital syndrome (AGS), also known as congenital adrenal hyperplasia (CAH) in which there is a deficiency of an adrenocortical enzyme steroid, 21-hydroxylase. This results in abnormal functioning of the adrenal glands and insufficient production of certain steroidal hormones (aldosterone, cortisol) and increased synthesis of others, namely androgens including testosterone. (Moir stops short of calling this actual male hormone such as androgen or testosterone, rather calling it, "a substance much akin to male hormone.") This produces male hormone exposure during fetal development, resulting in at least partial male patterning of the brain.

In genetic females, the exposure to male hormones (or male hormone look-alikes) may result in functional internal female reproductive organs coupled with either external sexually-ambiguous or male genitalia, though female gender identity is almost always maintained. However, these individuals may prefer to play with boys and boy's toys, and exhibit more boisterous or tomboyish behavior.

Higher testosterone levels at particular times during fetal development may lead to bisexuality or homosexuality. In about two percent of genetically female individuals, CAH results in fetal development of male gender identity during brain differentiation (Swaab, We Are Our Brains, pp. 59, 61).

Turner Syndrome

In an XX female fetus, the ovaries normally produce a slight amount of male hormone. In Turner Syndrome, the female has only one X sex chromosome, the other being absent or partially deleted. This is genetically designated as XO. She usually does not develop functioning ovaries. Lacking that small amount of male hormone, these women may develop ultra-female characteristics and exaggerated female behavior.

Maternal stress

Extreme conditions of stress in the pregnant mother have been shown to result in the brain of genetically male offspring developing with increased female characteristics, and genetically female offspring developing male brain characteristics. Stress in the mother increases her cortisol (stress hormone) levels, which in turn impacts fetal sex hormones and incidence of homosexuality in the offspring (Swaab, We Are Our Brains, p. 48).

Fetal exposure to endocrine disruptors

Many substances have been identified as endocrine-disrupting chemicals (EDCs): DDT (dichloro-diphenyl-trichloroethane, a synthetic insecticide developed in the 1940s and now banned worldwide), PCBs (polychlorinated biphenyl, synthetic compounds used in electrical equipment such as circuit boards and capacitors), dioxins (highly toxic compounds either manufactured or unintentionally produced as by-products of industrial processes or improper waste disposal), phthalates, and others. Due to their effects on hormones, EDCs can disrupt sexual differentiation during fetal development.

Phthalates are chemicals used in some plastics and personal care products, and can be present in food. Studies have shown phthalates to be EDCs that adversely affect the body's natural production of hormones.

Evan Koch, in the article "Study Links Exposure to Common Chemicals During Early Pregnancy to Altered Hormone Levels in Fetus," March 9, 2017, discusses results with phthalates study leader Dr. Sheela Sathyanarayana. Dr. Sathyanarayana is a pediatric environmental health specialist at Seattle Children's Research Institute and associate professor at the University of Washington.

Dr. Sathyanarayana's studies have shown that when a human fetus is exposed to phthalates during the first trimester of pregnancy, as EDCs they can produce elevated levels of estrogen and diminished production of testosterone. This can result in genital abnormalities and reproductive issues in males.

The report of the study, published in *The Journal of Clinical Endocrinology & Metabolism*, concludes that the degree of male genital abnormality is inversely proportional to the amount of male hormones present during fetal development. That is, the more that phthalates decrease the normal production of male hormones, the greater the likelihood that genital abnormalities will be evident at birth. This finding is consistent with that reported by Moir and Jessel.

As we have seen, a reduction in male hormones in the fetus also is likely to have feminized the patterning of the brain.

In Koch's article, Dr. Sathyanarayana indicates that there has been insufficient data to publish the effects of phthalates on female fetuses.

Note that, as with genetic differences in sex chromosome combinations, this may not be an exhaustive list of hormonal effects on a developing human fetus.

Drugs, chemicals, and sexual orientation

Several substances are known to affect brain structures related to sexual orientation. Studies and brain scans have shown that sexual orientation is associated (at a minimum) with the hypothalamus, amygdala connections with other portions of the brain, thalamus, and prefrontal cortex. As stated previously, these structural and functional brain differences develop during the second half of pregnancy (Swaab, We Are Our Brains, pp. 61 – 63).

Diethylstilbestrol (DES), a synthetic estrogen given to pregnant women, can affect development in the fetus of brain areas determining sexual orientation, increasing the likelihood of daughters becoming bisexual or lesbian.

Nicotine or amphetamine use in pregnant women affects brain areas related to sexual orientation, increasing the incidence of lesbian daughters.

A mother's immune response to a male fetus increases with each male child, correspondingly increasing the effect on each male child's brain structures associated with sexual orientation, and therefore the potential likelihood of homosexuality (Swaab, We Are Our Brains, p. 61).

It's Not Nurture

The case for nature and gender identity

The question of "nature versus nurture" in regard to sexual identity was thought, through the mid-twentieth century, to lean toward nurture – a child's gender identity would adapt to the circumstances in which they were raised.

The fallacy of this belief is evident in the story of a boy who was raised as a girl and later underwent the process of surgery and treatments to live as the man he knew he was. Journalist and author John Colapinto documented the boy's life in the New York Times bestseller *As Nature Made Him: The Boy Who Was Raised as a Girl*. After years of anonymity as the "John – Joan – John" case, David Reimer went public with his story in the attempt to prevent sexual assignment surgery in children before they are old enough to decide their gender identity for themselves. (He was born Bruce Reimer, but went by David after re-assignment surgery later in life.)

David (as well as his twin brother) was born with an abnormally small opening in the foreskin of his penis, which can cause difficult urination and potential kidney damage. At several months of age, David underwent corrective surgery. The intended minor correction was botched during the surgery when an intended blood vessel cauterization accidentally burned off his penis. (His brother's condition eventually corrected itself.) Months later, the boy's parents were persuaded to allow removal of the rest of the penis and testicles, and raise David as a girl, Brenda.

"Brenda" wore dresses, was given girl's toys, underwent psychological counselling (which included what might be considered bizarre, inappropriate, or even disturbing behavior on the part of the therapist), and was administered female hormones after reaching puberty. David always had felt male, not female, true to his male fetal brain patterning. By about age ten, he decidedly felt male. At age thirteen, he was told the truth of the matter. At age fifteen, he made the decision to live as a male. As a young adult, he went through gender re-assignment to be the man he had always known he was. He later married, adopting his wife's children.

The full story is too complex to detail here, but if you have any doubts that gender identity is truly based in nature and not nurture, read the book or Google the case. Wikipedia has a fairly extensive article, currently at https://en.wikipedia.org/wiki/David_Reimer.

Gender identity is hardwired into the brain during fetal development, based on genetics and the hormones and other chemicals to which a fetus is exposed in the womb.

Genetics and sexual orientation

The search for a "gay gene" to explain homosexuality has been ongoing for decades. Though portions of certain chromosomes have been associated with male homosexuality, the reality is more complex than a single "gay gene." We have discussed the effects of fetal exposure to male hormones and endocrine disrupting chemicals, and know that a complex combination of factors is involved. Here, we'll look at the genetics that have been well substantiated at the time of this writing. Note that no one has claimed to have identified a single "gay gene."

Several studies looked for differences in chromosomes between homosexual men and heterosexual men of the same family (Servick, 2014; Wikipedia, "Xq28," 2019). (These involved multiple families.) Several reports discuss the studies and results, and Wikipedia sums them up nicely in an article, "Biology and sexual orientation": In 1993 it was found that there was a difference at the end of the long arm of the X chromosome, location Xq28 (Hamer et al., 1993). A region of chromosome 8 (8p12) also has been identified, although a specific gene or genes have yet to be determined (Mustanski et al., 2005; Sanders et al., 2015). These regions have not been shown to be associated with female homosexuality.

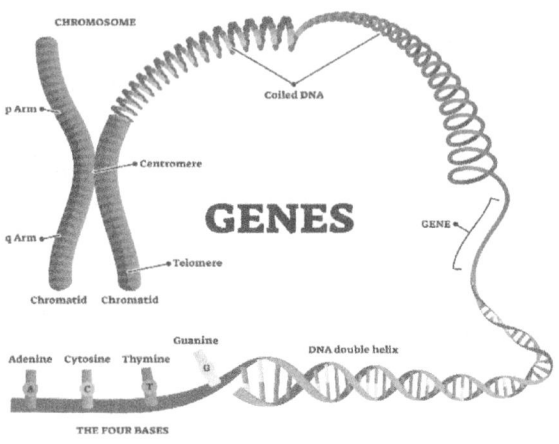

What does Xq28 mean, and where is it?

For the inquiring mind: the cytogenetic method of identifying gene locations on a chromosome in essence provides the neighborhood, but not the street address or apartment number.

Human chromosomes are numbered from 1 to 22 for the autosomes, in order from longest to shortest. The sex chromosomes are X and Y. Each chromosome has two arms (one shorter, one longer) joined by a centromere. The dark and light bands resulting from a particular type of staining are used to identify regions, bands, and sub-bands. Numbering of regions and bands begins at the centromere and increments as one moves toward each arm end (the telomere). In this convention of locating the neighborhood of a gene or genes, for Xq28:

1. The first number(s) or letter identifies the chromosome, in this case (Xq28), the X chromosome.
2. The next letter indicates if it's on the short arm (p) or the long arm (q) of the chromosome. Xq28 is on the long arm of chromosome X.
3. The third number is the region. Xq28 is in region 2, based on the light and dark patterns of staining.
4. The fourth number is the band. Xq28 is in the 8th band of region 2 on the long arm of chromosome X.
5. A sub-band to further narrow down the locations may be added after a decimal point. No sub-band is included in Xq28.

Now, back to our regularly scheduled programming.

X chromosome
(loose approximation)

Xq28

Note: Most of the illustrations of X chromosomes that I have found have differed in the way the bands are drawn. The above pattern is roughly based (and crudely represented here) on one provided by the National Institutes of Health, which I consider to be a credible resource. For a truly professional rendering, go to the National Institutes of Health article, "Genes and Disease" on the NCBI Bookshelf published by the National Center for Biotechnology Information, U.S. National Library of Medicine here https://www.ncbi.nlm.nih.gov/books/NBK22266/#A295, or find a nicely-detailed illustration in the Wikipedia "Xq28" article here https://en.wikipedia.org/wiki/Xq28. The "Genes and Disease" article includes illustrations of all the human chromosomes labeled with known diseases associated with specific locations on each.

***

Alan Sanders of North Shore University, Illinois, led a team who found potential associations with male homosexuality on chromosomes 13 and 14. Gene *SLITRK6* on chromosome 13 is implicated through its effect on the brain's diencephalon, which contains the hypothalamus. Chromosome 14 contains gene *TSHR*, which primarily affects the thyroid gland, being responsible for making the protein receptor for thyroid stimulating hormone (TSH). Both hypothyroidism and hyperthyroidism have been associated with sexual dysfunction symptoms, such as erectile dysfunction (ED) and others, so there appears to be a link between the thyroid gland and sexual function (Servick, 2014).

Ellis et al. (2008) found statistically disproportionate incidences of blood type A and negative Rh factor in homosexual males and homosexual females as compared to the general population. These findings implicate both chromosome 9 (in location 9q34), which is associated with blood type, and chromosome 1 (in location 1p36), which is associated with the Rh factor (Wikipedia, "Biology and sexual orientation," 2019).

Research to find genetic bases for sexual orientation is ongoing.

Nature and sexual orientation

Like gender identity, sexual orientation is set in brain structure prior to birth. It, too, is determined by a combination of genetics and fetal exposure to male hormones or endocrine disrupting chemicals. Degree of female versus male patterning is subject to the level and timing of these hormones or disruptors.

In *Our Creative Brains*, Dick Swaab sums up the case for letting nature take its course:

> Everything imaginable has been tried, without success, in efforts to turn homosexual men into heterosexuals. Hormone therapy, castration, testes transplants, psychological, neurological and psychiatric treatments: none of these has ever had any documented effect. The social environment after birth seems to have no impact on our sexual orientation.
>
> The example set by parents is not followed in this respect either. Children adopted by two lesbian mothers or two homosexual fathers are not any more likely to become homosexual than children brought up by heterosexual couples. We can conclude that the sexual orientation of the parents has no influence on the sexual orientation of the child. Such children do well in every respect.

Dr. Swaab further explains that any psychological differences in adoptees between the two groups has been found to favor children adopted by the homosexual parents, possibly because homosexual couples must be more highly motivated in order to adopt. "Nor is there any evidence for the notion that homosexuality is a lifestyle choice," he states.

Cases of ambiguity

Anatomical sexual ambiguity has been discussed in earlier chapters. For someone appearing ambiguous as to their gender identity and/or sexual orientation (or inconsistent between the two), the likely explanation is the mosaic of both male and female patterning in the various sexually differentiated brain structures. This could be due to either:

(a) a *mix* of male- and female-patterned structures resulting from differing levels of chemicals or male hormones throughout fetal development, or

(b) ambiguity *within* one or more of the sexually differentiated areas, resulting from lower levels of male hormones or from disrupting chemicals or drugs during that structure's development in the fetus.

The Biology of Sex and Gender

Defining "sex"

When speaking of "sex," is male versus female based on genetics – XX and XY? Or is it based on appearance of external genitalia? Or on the presence of internal reproductive organs? We have seen examples in which the genitalia belie the genetics. Sex chromosomes and external genitalia may be outright contradictory. There are cases in which the external genitalia and internal reproductive organs may not both represent the same sex.

A simple "birth sex" or "biological sex" interpretation of "sex" is inadequate. As we have seen, the matter can be complex, confusing, or ambiguous.

- An individual can be born with genetic combinations of sex chromosomes other than XX or XY, that is, XXY, XYY, XXYY, XO, or others.
- In an XX female, the physical presentation of reproductive organs and genitalia can be male.
- Similarly, an XY male can be born with female reproductive organs and genitalia.
- An individual may be born with ambiguous genitalia – not definitively either female or male.
- An individual may be born with partial or complete dual sets of sex organs representing both female and male.

These factors necessitate careful consideration in defining legal matters relevant to "sex."

Additionally to be considered is the sexually differentiated development of certain areas of the brain into a male pattern, a female pattern, or combination with some of each. This brain patterning is the biological basis for not only certain male versus female behaviors, but also gender identity and sexual orientation. It's set in the physical structure of the brain, and determines how the brain functions, its strengths, and its preferences. This is part of the biology of "sex."

Gender identity and sexual orientation

Attributes of gender identity and sexual orientation are determined by biological brain development and differentiation. Each has its basis in one or more specific areas of the hypothalamus and other brain structures. This patterning follows a mosaic concept, in which areas associated with gender identity or sexual orientation may be more male patterned, more female patterned, or mixed, with either attribute being more female and the other more male.

Each structure develops physically as instructed according to genetics and levels of male sex hormones (or their absence) during the embryonic and fetal stages of development, irrespective of genetic sex chromosomes.

Environmental factors such as endocrine-disrupting chemicals or stress on the mother while pregnant may also play a role.

These brain structures physically and functionally differ between male and female, where "male" and "female" may not match the sex chromosomes.

Gender identity as driven by patterning of sexually-differentiating brain structures may or may not agree with the individual's physical equipment. These various bits – the internal and external sex structures, as well as the brain structures – may not match one another in terms of sex, or may have developed ambiguously. It's even possible for the internal reproductive organs to differ from the external anatomical representation. Sex chromosome configuration combined with fluctuations in sex hormones during fetal development can create an array of results.

Depending on the degree of maleness versus femaleness in each sexually-differentiated brain structure, a person identifying as male (irrespective of their sex chromosomes or sexual anatomy) may choose either male or female sexual partners. Or both (bisexual). Or neither.

Similarly, a person identifying as female (irrespective of their sex chromosomes or sexual anatomy) may choose either male or female partners. Or both (bisexual). Or neither. It's all a matter of degree, based on biological structure and function within the brain, which was driven by level and timing of fetal exposure to sex hormones or chemicals mimicking them.

Though some people identify as L, G, B, T, Q, or I from early childhood, some factors may not kick in until puberty, depending on the root biological functions affected. Remember, this is not an "on" or "off" switch; it's not black or white – there's a whole range of development, an entire continuum between female and male brain patterning. Gender identity can be anywhere within that range. Sexual orientation can be anywhere within that range. And the two can be independent of one another.

The biology is fairly simple to understand, though research still is determining involvement of genetics, as well as specific brain structures and their functions. The wide ranges in physical structure and function of multiple areas in the brain that affect sexuality create many variations in results.

There are a myriad of biological paths to sex definition and development. Gender identity is not a choice. Sexual orientation is not something to be cured.

Indeed, studies have proven that once past fetal development, exposure to female hormones will not restructure a male-patterned brain into a female pattern. Male hormones will not restructure an adult female-patterned brain into a male pattern.

Sex hormones in adults may, however, impact anatomical attributes such as hair growth and breast development, or behavioral tendencies such as being aggressive versus passive.

We have seen now that gender identity and sexual orientation have a biological basis, and may be determined independently of one another. They result from the genetics (sex chromosomes and perhaps specific regions of certain autosomes) in combination with the physical brain patterning and its resulting functions.

Those genetic factors and structural brain characteristics, along with both internal and external anatomy, combine different aspects of an individual's biological sex.

We are not living in a binary male versus female, all black and white world. The biological paths to sex, gender identity, and sexual orientation are many and varied. They develop on a colorful spectrum that is not a choice.

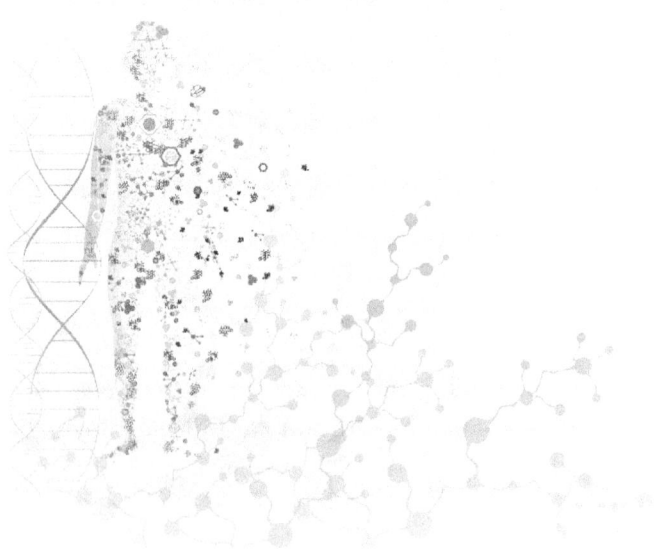

Commentary

We, all of us, are worthy of civil rights protections.

If we're simply accidents of nature, we're all accidents of nature, subject to the whimsical rolls of Nature's dice.

If we're all creations of a higher power, then isn't each of us molded with a particular purpose in mind? We may not know what ours is, and certainly nobody else knows. At least, not until we discover and display it for others to see.

Either way, while each of us is unique, we all are equal. We all deserve life, liberty, and the pursuit of happiness. We all deserve equal protections under the law.

Each of us is beholden to treat others as we would wish to be treated. Watching others treat someone badly does not make it alright for them, or you, or anyone else to do so. If someone disrespects you, you do not need to disrespect another in return. Hold your head high, and respect yourself enough to do what you know in your heart is right – and continue to treat others with respect.

Being different does not make a person less deserving than you. Being different, or someone "other" than you, simply means you don't know them. You can learn. Remember, you are "other" to them, too. You can teach them about yourself, but don't you want to show them that as their "other" you have a good side? Show the positive, the caring, the respectful. You probably would like them to accept and respect you, too. Be your best self, and let others be theirs.

No one truly gains by stripping others of their legislated or god-given inalienable rights. In unfounded persecution, everyone loses – those doing the persecuting as much as the persecuted.

Rather than spending time and effort excluding or persecuting those different from ourselves, our time and efforts would be better spent learning from those whose life experiences might add to our own. We'd create a more productive synergy by combining our efforts in pursuit of more positive goals - ones in which we all win.

***

Please consider leaving a review on Amazon:
https://www.amazon.com/dp/B07XK8HKQT or
https://www.amazon.com/dp/ 0976323516/

If you have a question, suggestion, or request, please contact us from the website:
https://notachoice.net/contact/

Sign up on our website for updates (about once a year) and a **free pdf article:**
https://notachoice.net/free-articles/

We do not share contact information.

Postscript

A few weeks after completion of this book, I came across a CNN article written by Aisha Salaudeen, dated September 22, 2019: "Growing up intersex in a country where it is believed to be bad luck," published in CNN's *Inside Africa* column. While my book is focused on the biological nature of female versus male and all the in-betweens, Salaudeen's article details the physical, emotional, and social effects experienced by specific individuals, Babalwa Mtshawu and others. Babalwa was born in South Africa with female external genitalia and male internal sex organs. The discrepancy became evident upon examination by a physician after sexual development at puberty failed to proceed as female.

Intersex individuals are those whose birth genitalia, reproductive organs, sex chromosomes, and/or sex hormones are atypical, falling outside the specific definitions of female or male, and may represent as much as 2% of the world population. At a current population of 7.7 billion, that's 154,000,000 people who could be intersex. That's about the same as the number of people born with naturally red hair.

My takeaways from Salaudeen's article are these:
- South Africa's constitution mandates gender and sexual diversity education.
- Mtshawu advocates for intersex education, hoping to dispel misconceptions about the variety of conditions it encompasses.

- The article quotes Mtshawu:

  > The curriculum is slowly changing in South Africa, and I think it will be easy for them to teach intersex because <u>it is just plain biology</u>. This is a natural phenomenon, like someone being born without an arm or having an extra finger.

  Underlining is mine. This is exactly the point that I'm making with this book.

- South Africa enacted laws protecting the rights of intersex people.
- According to Salaudeen, South Africa's "Sex Description Act of 2003 legally recognizes intersex persons and allows them to alter their name and sex on birth certificates to suit their preferred gender role."

I have read South Africa's "Alteration of Sex Description and Sex Status Act, 2003," and am including it in Appendix D.

Additionally, I have reviewed South Africa's "Promotion of Equality and Prevention of Unfair Discrimination Act 4 of 2000," with its amendments up through 2008. An explicit definition of "intersex" was added in 2005: *"intersex means a congenital sexual differentiation which is atypical, to whatever degree."*

The Act's definition of "prohibited grounds" in the context of protection from discrimination explicitly includes sexual orientation as well as gender and sex:

'prohibited grounds' are-

(a) race, gender, sex, pregnancy, marital status, ethnic or social origin, colour, sexual orientation, age, disability, religion, conscience, belief, culture, language and birth; or

(b) any other ground where discrimination based on that ground-

> (i) causes or perpetuates systemic disadvantage;
>
> (ii) undermines human dignity; or
>
> (iii) adversely affects the equal enjoyment of a person's rights and freedoms in a serious manner that is comparable to discrimination on a ground in paragraph (a).

The definition of "sex" explicitly includes intersex:

> 'sex' includes intersex;
>
> [Definition of "sex" inserted by s. 16 (b) of Act 22 of 2005.]

My question is this: Why is South Africa more progressive in providing legal recognition for non-binary individuals than is the United States?

Aisha Salaudeen's article includes statements by Dr. David Segal. Dr. Segal is a paediatric endocrinologist and diabetologist in Johannesburg, South Africa. He specializes in the function of glands and hormones. Endocrine glands include the hypothalamus, adrenal glands, ovaries, and testes (which we have discussed), as well as pituitary, thyroid, parathyroid, and pancreas, among others. According to Salaudeen, Dr. Segal believes that intersex individuals experience discrimination, "because society does not have enough public information on intersexuality."

Dr. Segal: "We are used to contrast. It's either one is short or tall, skinny or fat, male or female, there's no in-between and no consideration for other options. *There is no biological understanding of what's going on. If people understood it they wouldn't discriminate.*" (Italics are mine.)

Along with helping intersex individuals and others in the LGBTQ community to understand the "whys and hows" and to be more comfortable with themselves, those last two sentences of Dr. Segal's are the exact reason I wrote this book!

South Africa is not alone in providing legal protections for people who are intersex. According to an article published by the Thomson Reuters Foundation in June 2016, Great Britain, Bolivia, Ecuador, Fiji, and Malta provide equal constitutional rights for LGBT people.

Germany has allowed the birth certificate male/female choice to be left blank since 2013. December 14, 2018, the German parliament passed into law a provision for "miscellaneous" to be entered on the birth certificate for intersex newborns. It is also possible to change the sex on the birth certificate later, after medical examination.

November 2018, the top court (the Federal Constitutional Court) ruled on an issue of discrimination against intersex individuals, noting that sexual identity is protected as a basic right.

I ask again: Why is the United States so slow to recognize non-binary, intersex people; update the definition of "sex" to reflect the biological reality; and explicitly grant legal protections to this group of people?

PJ Paulson
September 23, 2019

About the Author

PJ Paulson practices social distancing among cats, dogs, and interesting neighbors on the high plains of Colorado, where horses and white-faced cattle are backdropped against sage-green hills, purple snow-capped mountains, and salmon sunsets.

Acknowledgements

First and foremost, a heartfelt and enthusiastic, "Thank you!" to Dick Swaab. Dr. Swaab provided me with new material from his team's most recent research as of October 2019, as well as a 2019 English translation of his recent book, *Our Creative Brains: How World and Mankind Shape Each Other*. I find both his new and previous book, *We Are Our Brains: From the Womb to Alzheimer's*, absolutely fascinating and heartily recommend them. Though busy with his continued research, Dr. Swaab has graciously taken time to offer both information and support for this book. In February 2021, he added another brain structure associated with being transgender / transsexual. Again, thank you!

I want to thank two insightful and supportive friends, both of whom possess amazing technical and emotional support skills. Half a world apart, each with their special contributions helped me find my way through the decisions to be made between First Draft and Publish.

Special thanks to Linda for cover design. After my repeated posts requesting feedback on cover after cover (none of which felt right), I imagine Linda decided it was time to set me on a different path. She sent me a prototype that clicked, and when finished it finally felt right.

With much gratitude, I thank both Linda and Eric for critiquing early drafts. Your suggestions have wrought improvements. Your enthusiasm is the icing on the cake!

Thank you!
PJ

Appendix A: Gene Mutations, Sex Reversal, and Gonadal Dysgenesis

Sex reversal

Sex reversal is defined by Wikipedia as, "a biological process whereby the pathway directed towards the already determined-sex fate is flipped towards the opposite sex, creating a discordance between the primary sex fate and the sex phenotype expressed." (https://en.wikipedia.org/wiki/Sex_reversal, February 5, 2021). Phenotype represents the physical expression of the genes, or an aspect of the individual's appearance. Basically, the sex organs develop in a manner contrary to what would be expected based on the sex chromosomes of the individual. Simply put, a genetic male fetus is born with female sex organs, or a genetic female fetus is born with male sex organs.

Gonadal dysgenesis

Gonadal dysgenesis is atypical (not typical) development of gonads in the fetus. They could be of the opposite sex as in sex reversal, a mix of male and female, or incompletely developed to varying degrees.

Both sex reversal and gonadal dysgenesis may be attributed to multiple factors. The focus in this appendix is on a representative subset of gene mutations known to cause a few of the many forms of reversal or dysgenesis.

Gene locations

For reference when locating genes whose mutations are discussed below: Each chromosome includes a shorter arm, designated as "p", and a longer arm, designated as "q", when mapping gene locations using cytogenetic bands. The arms are connected at the centromere; the ends of the arms are the telomeres. Regions and bands are numbered sequentially on each arm beginning at the centromere and incrementing the numbers while moving toward the telomere ends.

MAP3K1 and Swyer Syndrome

Mutations to certain genes are known to result in certain intersex conditions. In Swyer Syndrome, a type of gonadal dysgenesis, an XY male appears female at birth, develops with female sex characteristics, but lacks functioning ovaries. These individuals usually are raised as girls, and may be able to give birth with donated eggs or embryos. SRY gene mutations account for about 15% of Swyer Syndrome cases.

MAP3K1 gene mutations account for up to 18% of Swyer Syndrome cases. MAP3K1 is a protein coding gene located at cytogenetic band 5q11.2, which translates to chromosome 5, long arm, region 1, band 1, sub-band 2. This places it close to the centromere (the point at which the long and short arms of the chromosome are connected). MAP3K1 mutations have been associated with both 46,XY Sex Reversal 6 and 46,XY Partial Gonadal Dysgenesis.

DHH and NR5A1

Mutations to DHH and NR5A1 account for a smaller number of Swyer Syndrome cases. DHH is a protein coding gene that has been associated with 46,XY Sex Reversal 7 and 46,XY Gonadal Dysgenesis, Partial, With Minifascicular Neuropathy. It is located at 12q13.12: chromosome 12, long arm, region 1, band 3, sub-band 12.

NR5A1 (Nuclear Receptor Subfamily 5 Group A Member 1) is located on chromosome 9 at 9q33.3: chromosome 9, long arm, region 3, band 3, sub-band 3. It is a protein coding gene whose mutations are associated with both 46,XY Sex Reversal 3 in genetic males (sex reversal; gonadal dysgenesis; failure to develop secondary sex characteristics at puberty; and occasionally clitoral hypertrophy, labial fusion, dysgenetic testes, hypoplasia of the uterus, or ambiguous genitalia) and 46,XX Sex Reversal 4 in genetic females (development of male gonads, micropenis, ambiguous genitalia, clitoral hypertrophy, clitoromegaly, rugated labia majora, ovotestes, short blind-ending vagina, small penis, retractile testes, atrophic testes, dysgenetic testes, or penoscrotal hypospadias, as well as other effects).

These gene mutations generally have multiple effects on development of the fetus, such as adrenal failure or corticoadrenal insufficiency, in addition to their effects on sexual development. For our purpose, the focus is on the aspect of sexual development. Some of the gene mutations affect production of steroidal hormones and therefore sexual development and male-female brain differentiation in the fetus through those hormonal influences.

SOX3, SOX9, SRXY10

Mutations of the SOX3 gene may cause male gonads to develop in a genetic female in what is known as a female-to-male sex reversal. SOX3 is located on the X chromosome at Xq27.1, which is on the long arm of the X chromosome and closer to the end (telomere) than to the middle (centromere): X chromosome, long arm, region 2, band 7, sub-band 1.

SRXY10 gene mutation is associated with 46,XY sex reversal (also known as chromosome 17q24 deletion syndrome), in which a genetic male develops female genitalia, but does not develop secondary sex characteristics at puberty. SRXY10 is located at 17q24, which is on the long arm of chromosome 17, closer to the end than the middle: chromosome 17, long arm, region 2, band 4. The SOX9 gene also is located in band 17q24. Mutations to both SRXY10 and SOX9 are associated with 46,XY Sex Reversal 10.

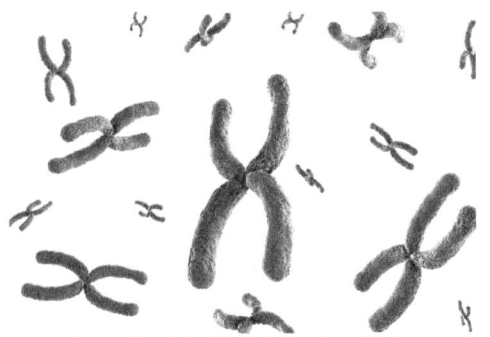

Image © Adobe Stock / phonlamaiphoto

Appendix B: Reducing Phthalate Exposure

In his March 9, 2017 *On the Pulse* article, "Study Links Exposure to Common Chemicals During Early Pregnancy to Altered Hormone Levels in Fetus," Evan Koch asks Dr. Sheela Sathyanarayana for his advice on how expecting mothers can avoid phthalate exposure. The response is summarized below.

Products made of plastic or vinyl often are softened and made more flexible by the addition of phthalates. These can leach into food and thus be consumed. Environmental sources include flooring, wall coverings, and personal care products (shampoos, lotions, etc.). Try to reduce phthalate exposure as follows:

- Use items labeled phthalate-free or BPA-free. Avoid containers displaying the following symbols:
    - 3 inside a triangle indicates V or PVC, which is vinyl (contains phthalates)
    - 6 inside a triangle, indicating Styrofoam or polystyrene
    - 7 in a triangle indicates miscellaneous plastics, which can contain bisphenol-A (BPA), a harmful toxin
- Use personal care products made with natural ingredients and free of added chemicals. Look for those packaged in glass containers or plastic that is designated BPA-free or phthalate-free.

- Avoid serving, eating, or storing food in plastics. Use alternate materials (glass, stainless steel, ceramic, wood). Never microwave food or drinks in plastic. This is especially important when preparing food or drinks for infants and small children.
- Use low-fat rather than high-fat dairy products.
- Eat fresh or frozen foods rather than canned or processed.
- Remove shoes at home to avoid tracking in dust or other phthalate-containing materials.
- Clean home surfaces (carpets, windowsills, etc.) to avoid collecting phthalates.
- Wash hands frequently.

Appendix C: Excerpt from the Civil Rights Act of 1964, Title VII

(a) Employer practices

It shall be an unlawful employment practice for an employer –

(1) to fail or refuse to hire or to discharge any individual, or otherwise to discriminate against any individual with respect to his compensation, terms, conditions, or privileges of employment, because of such individual's race, color, religion, sex, or national origin; or

(2) to limit, segregate, or classify his employees or applicants for employment in any way which would deprive or tend to deprive any individual of employment opportunities or otherwise adversely affect his status as an employee, because of such individual's race, color, religion, sex, or national origin.

Appendix D: South Africa's Alteration of Sex Description and Sex Status Act, 2003

Government Gazette

REPUBLIC OF SOUTH AFRICA

Vol. 465 Cape Town 15 March 2004 No. 26148

THE PRESIDENCY

No. 331 15 March 2004

It is hereby notified that the President has assented to the following Act, which is hereby published for general information:–

No. 49 of 2003: Alteration of Sex Description and Sex Status Act, 2003.

Act No. 49,2003 ALTERATION OF SEX DESCRIPTION AND SEX STATUS ACT, 2003

GENERAL EXPLANATORY NOTE:

Words underlined with a solid line indicate insertions in existing enactments.

(English text signed by the President.)
(Assented to 9 March 2004.)

ACT

To provide for the alteration of the sex description of certain individuals in certain circumstances; and to amend the Births and Deaths Registration Act, 1992, as a consequence; and to provide for matters incidental thereto.

BE IT ENACTED by the Parliament of the Republic of South Africa, as follows:-

Definitions

1. In this Act, unless the context indicates otherwise-

"gender characteristics" means the ways in which a person expresses his or her social identity as a member of a particular sex by using style of dressing, the wearing of prostheses or other means;

"gender reassignment" means a process which is undertaken for the purpose of reassigning a person's sex by changing physiological or other sexual characteristics, and includes any part of such a process;

"intersexed", with reference to a person, means a person whose congenital sexual differentiation is atypical, to whatever degree;

"medical practitioner" means a person providing health services in terms of any law, including in terms of the-

(a) Allied Health Professions Act, 1982 (Act No. 63 of 1982);

(b) Health Professions Act, 1974 (Act No. 56 of 1974);

(c) Nursing Act, 1978 (Act No. 50 of 1978);

(d) Pharmacy Act, 1974 (Act No. 53 of 1974);

(e) Dental Technicians Act, 1979 (Act No. 19 of 1979); and

(f) Mental Health Care Act, 2002 (Act No. 17 of 2002);

"primary sexual characteristics" means the form of the genitalia at birth;

"secondary sexual characteristics" means those which develop throughout life and which are dependant [sic] upon the hormonal base of the individual person;

"sexual characteristics" means primary or secondary sexual characteristics or gender characteristics.

Application for alteration of sex description

2. (1) Any person whose sexual characteristics have been altered by surgical or medical treatment or by evolvement through natural development resulting in gender reassignment, or any person who is intersexed may apply to the Director-General of the National Department of Home Affairs for the alteration of the sex description on his or her birth register.

(2) An application contemplated in subsection (1) must-

> *(a)* be accompanied by the birth certificate of the applicant;
> *(b)* in the case of a person whose sexual characteristics have been altered by surgical or medical treatment resulting in gender reassignment, be accompanied by reports stating the nature and results of any procedures carried out and any treatment applied prepared by the medical practitioners who carried out the procedures and applied the treatment or by a medical practitioner with experience in the carrying out of such procedures and the application of such treatment;
> *(c)* in every case in which sexual characteristics have been altered resulting in gender reassignment, be accompanied by a report prepared by a medical practitioner other than the one contemplated in paragraph *(b)* who has medically examined the applicant in order to establish his or her sexual characteristics; and
> *(d)* in the case of a person who is intersexed, be accompanied by-

>> (i) a report 'prepared by a medical practitioner corroborating that the applicant is intersexed; and
>> (ii) a report prepared by a qualified psychologist or social worker corroborating that the applicant is living and has lived stably and satisfactorily for an unbroken period of at least two years, in the

gender role corresponding to the sex description under which he or she seeks to be registered.

(3) If the Director-General refuses the application contemplated in subsection (1), he or she must furnish the applicant with written reasons for the decision.

(4) If an application contemplated in subsection (1) is refused, the applicant may appeal to the Minister of Home Affairs against the decision taken by the Director-General.

(5) An application contemplated in subsection (4) must be lodged with the Minister within 14 days after the decision of the Director-General was made known and must be accompanied by the documents referred to in subsection (2) and the reasons for the Director-General's refusal.

(6) If an appeal in terms of subsection (4) is refused, the applicant may apply to the magistrate of the district in which he or she resides for an order directing the change of his or her sex description.

(7) An application contemplated in subsection (6) must be accompanied by the documents referred to in subsection (2) and the reasons for the Minister's refusal.

(8) On the date and at the time determined by the magistrate the applicant must appear before the magistrate in chambers and must at the request of the magistrate furnish such additional information and proof as the magistrate may require.

(9) If the application is granted the magistrate must issue an order directing the Director-General to alter the sex description in the birth register of the person named in the order.

(10) An applicant may, on his or her appearance before the magistrate, be assisted by a legal representative.

Order for alteration of sex description

3. (1) If the Director-General grants an application contemplated in section 2(1) or receives an order from a magistrate in terms of section 2(9), the Director-General must proceed in terms of section 27A of the Births and Deaths Registration Act, 1992 (Act No. 51 of 1992).

(2) A person whose sex description has been altered, is deemed for all purposes to be a person of the sex description so altered as from the date of the recording of such alteration.

(3) Rights and obligations that have been acquired by or accrued to such a person before the alteration of his or her sex description are not adversely affected by the alteration.

Insertion of section 27A in Act 51 of 1992

4. The following section is hereby inserted in the Births and Deaths Registration Act, 1992, after section 27:

"Alteration of sex description

27A. (1) If the Director-General grants an application or a magistrate issues an order in terms of section 2 of the Alteration of Sex Description and Sex Status Act, 2003, the Director-General shall alter the sex description on the birth register of the person concerned.
(2) An alteration so recorded shall be dated and after the recording of the said alteration the person concerned shall be entitled to be issued with an amended birth certificate.".

Short title

5. This Act is called the Alteration of Sex Description and Sex Status Act, 2003.

Appendix E: Don't Know Where to Turn? Try PFLAG

If you need someone who understands and can relate, you might start with PFLAG. Locate a chapter near you here: https://pflag.org/find-a-chapter.

PFLAG began as Parents and Friends of Lesbians and Gays; it later was changed to Parents, Families and Friends of Lesbians and Gays; and eventually (2014 according to Wikipedia) the acronym became the actual name of the organization.

From their website:
PFLAG is the first and largest organization for lesbian, gay, bisexual, transgender, and queer (LGBTQ+) people, their parents and families, and allies. With over 400 chapters and 200,000 members and supporters crossing multiple generations of families in major urban centers, small cities, and rural areas across America, PFLAG is committed to creating a world where diversity is celebrated and all people are respected, valued, and affirmed.

This vast grassroots network is cultivated, resourced, and serviced by the staff of PFLAG National, the National Board of Directors, and the all-volunteer Regional Directors Council.

To learn more, visit https://pflag.org/, like us on Facebook (https://www.facebook.com/PFLAG/), or follow us on Twitter (<u>https://twitter.com/pflag</u>) @pflag or Instagram.

* * *

When I finished writing this book, I reached out to many, many organizations, both locally and worldwide, looking for people whom the information in it might help. The only organization from which someone responded was a local chapter of PFLAG. From them, I got a sense of open arms, open minds, and warm hearts. May you find the same!

Best Wishes to You!
PJ

Image © Shutterstock / Reenya

References

Ahn, Janice Y., J.T. Lee. "X Chromosome: X Inactivation," 2008. *X Chromosome Inactivation | Learn Science at Scitable.* Nature Education. Web. February 1, 2020.
<https://www.nature.com/scitable/topicpage/x-chromosome-x-inactivation-323/>

AXYS, "About 47,XXY (Klinefelter syndrome)," 2016. *About 47,XXY|The Association for X and Y Chromosome Variations.* AXYS. Web. February 24, 2020.
<https://genetic.org/variations/about-47xxy/?gclid=EAIaIQobChMIguKL27Lo5wIVKRitBh oZKQUgEAAYAiAAEgLYoPD_BwE>

Berletch, Joel B, Fan Yang, Jun Xu, Laura Carrel, & Christine M. Disteche. "Genes that escape from X inactivation," May 26, 2011. *Genes that escape from X inactivation.* US National Library of Medicine, National Institutes of Health. Web. December 26, 2019.
<https://www.ncbi.nlm.nih.gov/pmc/articles/PMC3136 209/>

Conklin, Jamie. "Chromosomes," January 7, 2019. *Understanding Genetics.* Stanford University, Stanford School of Medicine, Department of Genetics, The Tech Interactive. Web. February 9, 2020.
<https://genetics.thetech.org/ask/ask295>

Coughlan, Andy. "What do the new 'gay genes' tell us about sexual orientation?" December 7, 2017. *What do the new 'gay genes' tell us about sexual orientation? | New … .* Newscientist.com. Web. December 31, 2019. <https://www.newscientist.com/article/2155810-what-do-the-new-gay-genes-tell-us-about-sexual-orientation/>

eNCA. "German law allows third gender in birth certificates," December 14, 2018. *German law allows third gender in birth certificates | eNCA.* eNews Channel Africa (eNCA). Web. September 23, 2019. <https://www.enca.com/news/german-law-allows-third-gender-birth-certificates>

Genetics Home Reference: Your Guide to Understanding Genetic Conditions. "How do geneticists indicate the location of a gene?" January 21, 2020. *How do geneticists indicate the location of a gene – Genetics Hom….* US National Library of Medicine. Web. January 31, 2019. <https://ghr.nlm.nih.gov/primer/howgeneswork/genelocation>

Genetics Home Reference: Your Guide to Understanding Genetic Conditions. "Triple X syndrome," June 2014 (last reviewed); August 20, 2019 (web site updated). *Triple X syndrome – Genetics Home Reference – NIH.* US National Library of Medicine. Web. August 25, 2019. <https://ghr.nlm.nih.gov/condition/triple-x-syndrome>

Genetics Home Reference: Your Guide to Understanding Genetic Conditions. "Turner syndrome," October 2017 (last reviewed); August 20, 2019 (web site updated). *Turner syndrome – Genetics Home Reference – NIH*. US National Library of Medicine. Web. August 25, 2019. <https://ghr.nlm.nih.gov/condition/turner-syndrome#>

Genetics Home Reference. "46,XX testicular disorder of sex development." January 21, 2020. *46,XX testicular disorder of sex development – Genetics Home....* Lister Hill National Center for Biomedical Communications, US National Library of Medicine, National Institutes of Health, Department of Health & Human Services. Web. February 7, 2020. <https://ghr.nlm.nih.gov/condition/46xx-testicular-disorder-of-sex-development#genes>

Goldman, Bruce. "Two Minds: the cognitive differences between men and women," Spring 2017. *How men's and women's brains are different*. Stanford Medicine. Web. August 21, 2019. <https://stanmed.stanford.edu/2017spring/how-mens-and-womens-brains-are-different.html>

Gorski, R. A., Gordon, J. H., Shryne, J. E., and Southam, A. M. (1978). Evidence for a morphological sex difference within the medial preoptic area of the rat brain. Brain Res. 148, 333–346.

Green, Emma. "Why Trump Is Rolling Back LGBTQ Health-Care Protections," May 24, 2019. *Trump's Rollback of LGBTQ Protections in Obamacare – The Atlantic.* The Atlantic. Web. August 21, 2019. <https://www.theatlantic.com/politics/archive/2019/05/trumps-rollback-lgbtq-protections-obamacare/590239/>

IUPUI. "Meiosis and Formation of Eggs and Sperm," February 16, 2000. *Meiosis and Formation of Eggs and Sperm.* IUPUI Department of Biology. Web. December 31, 2019. <https://www.biology.iupui.edu/biocourses/N100H/ch9meiosis.html>

Joel, Daphna, Alicia Garcia-Falgueras, and Dick Swaab. "The Complex Relationships between Sex and the Brain," The Neuroscientist, I-14 (2019).

Joel, Daphna et al., "Sex beyond the genitalia: The human brain mosaic," November 30, 2015. *Sex beyond the genitalia: The human brain mosaic | PNAS.* Web. January 29, 2020. <https://www.pnas.org/content/112/50/15468>

Koch, Evan. "Study Links Exposure to Common Chemicals During Early Pregnancy to Altered Hormone Levels in Fetus," March 9, 2017. *Study Links Exposure to Common Chemicals During Early Pregnancy to Altered Hormone Levels in Fetus | On the Pulse.* Seattle Children's Hospital Research Foundation, On the Pulse.

<https://pulse.seattlechildrens.org/study-links-exposure-to-common-chemicals-during-early-pregnancy-to-altered-hormone-levels-in-fetus-that-can-lead-to-genital-abnormalities-in-boys/>

Koppens, PF; Hoogenboezem, T; Degenhart, HJ. "Adrenogenital syndrome. I. Introduction, enzymology, and heredity" [translated from Dutch], August 1989. *[Adrenogenital syndrome. I. Introduction, enzymology, and heredity]* – *PubMed* – *NCBI*. PubMed.gov, US National Library of Medicine, National Institutes of Health. Web. August 25, 2019.
<https://www.ncbi.nlm.nih.gov/pubmed/2678599>

Kruijver, F. P. M., Zhou, J. N., Pool, C. W., Hofman, M. A., Gooren, L. J. G., and Swaab, D. F. (2000). Male-to-female transsexuals have female neuron numbers in a limbic nucleus. J. Clin. Endocrinol. Metab. 85, 2034–2041.

Leblanc, Rick. "What Do Recycling Symbols Mean?" January 19, 2019. *What Do Recycling Symbols Mean?* The Balance Small Business. Web. September 5, 2019.
<https://www.thebalancesmb.com/what-recycling-symbols-mean-4126251#targetText=The%20%221%22%20inside%20a%20triangle,butter%20containers%2C%20and%20mouth wash%20bottles.>

LeVay, Simon. *Gay, Straight, and the Reason Why: The Science of Sexual Orientation.* 2011. New York. Oxford University Press.

LeVay, Simon. *Gay, Straight, and the Reason Why: The Science of Sexual Orientation, second edition.* 2016. New York. Oxford University Press.

Moir, Anne and Jessel, David. *Brain Sex: The Real Difference between Men & Women.* 1991. New York, NY: Carol Publishing Group.

National Institutes of Health. "Swyer Syndrome," January 1`, 2020. *Genetics Home Reference – Genetics – NIH.* Lister Hill National Center for Biomedical Communications, US National Library of Medicine, National Institutes of Health, Department of Health & Human Services. Web. February 7, 2020. <https://ghr.nlm.nih.gov/condition/swyer-syndrome#genes>

NCBI. "Genes and Disease." 1998. Updated January 31, 2011. *Chromosome Map – Genes and Disease – NCBI Bookshelf.* National Center for Biotechnology Information (NCBI), U.S. National Library of Medicine, National Institutes of Health. Web. February 4, 2020. <https://www.ncbi.nlm.nih.gov/books/NBK22266/#A295>

NCBI. "SRY Gene." January 21, 2020. *SRY Gene – Genetics Home Reference – NIH.* National Center for Biotechnology Information (NCBI), U.S. National Library of Medicine, National Institutes of Health. Web. February 7, 2020. <https://ghr.nlm.nih.gov/gene/SRY#synonyms>

NIH, "Congenital radioulnar synostosis," July 11, 2017. *Congenital radioulnar synostosis | Genetic and Rare Diseases ....* NIH (National Institutes of Health), National Center for Advancing Translational Sciences, Genetic and Rare Diseases Information Center (GARD). Web. February 24, 2020. <https://rarediseases.info.nih.gov/diseases/10876/congenital-radioulnar-synostosis>

Powell-Hamilton, Nina N. "Triple X Syndrome." November 2018. *Triple X Syndrome – Children's Health Issues – Merck Manuals Consumer Version.* Merck. Web. August 21, 2019. <https://www.merckmanuals.com/home/children-s-health-issues/chromosome-and-gene-abnormalities/triple-x-syndrome>

Powell-Hamilton, Nina N. "Klinefelter Syndrome." November 2018. *Klinefelter Syndrome – Children's Health Issues – Merck Manuals Consumer Version.* Merck. Web. August 21, 2019. <https://www.merckmanuals.com/home/children-s-health-issues/chromosome-and-gene-abnormalities/klinefelter-syndrome?query=klinefelter%20syndrome>

Powell-Hamilton, Nina N. "Turner Syndrome." November 2018. *Turner Syndrome – Children's Health Issues – Merck Manuals Consumer Version.* Merck. Web. August 21, 2019. <https://www.merckmanuals.com/home/children-s-health-issues/chromosome-and-gene-

abnormalities/turner-syndrome?query=turner%20syndrome>

Powell-Hamilton, Nina N. "XYY Syndrome." November 2018. *XYY Syndrome – Children's Health Issues – Merck Manuals Consumer Version.* Merck. Web. August 21, 2019. <https://www.merckmanuals.com/home/children-s-health-issues/chromosome-and-gene-abnormalities/xyy-syndrome?query=xyy%20syndrome>

PubMed. "Extreme skewing of X chromosome inactivation in mothers of homosexual men." December 21, 2005. *Extreme skewing of X chromosome inactivation in mothers of* .... NCBI, US National Library of Medicine, National Institutes of Health, PubMed.gov. Web. February 8, 2020. <https://www.ncbi.nlm.nih.gov/pubmed/16369763>

Republic of South Africa. "Alteration of Sex Description and Sex Status Act, 2003." March 15, 2004. *Alteration of Sex Description and Sex Status Act [No. 49 of 2003].* Government Gazette, Vol. 465, No. 26148. The Presidency, Cape Town, South Africa. Web. September 23, 2019. <https://www.gov.za/sites/default/files/gcis_document/201409/a49-03.pdf>

Republic of South Africa. "Promotion of Equality and Prevention of Unfair Discrimination Act 4 of 2000." English text signed by the President. February 2, 2000. <http://juta/nxt/print.asp?NXTScript=nxt/gateway.dll

&NXTHost=jut. Republic of South Africa. Web. September 23, 2019. <https://www.justice.gov.za/legislation/acts/2000-004.pdf>

Salaudeen, Aisha. "Growing up intersex in a country where it is believed to be bad luck." September 22, 2019. *Growing up intersex in a country where it is believed to be bad luck – CNN.* CNN – Inside Africa. Web. September 23, 2019. <https://www.cnn.com/2019/09/21/health/intersex-south-africa-intl/index.html>

Servick, Kelly. "Study of gay brothers may confirm X chromosome link to homosexuality." November 17, 2014. *Study of gay brothers may confirm X chromosome link to* .... Sciencemag.org. Web. December 31, 2019. <https://www.sciencemag.org/news/2014/11/study-gay-brothers-may-confirm-x-chromosome-link-homosexuality>

Sopelsa, Brooke, "Gay workers not covered by civil rights law, Trump admin tells Supreme Court," August 23, 2019. *Gay workers not covered by civil rights law, Trump admin tells Supreme Court.* NBC News. Web. August 25, 2019. <https://www.nbcnews.com/feature/nbc-out/gay-workers-not-covered-civil-rights-law-trump-admin-tells-n1045971>

Speer, Marcy C., "Crossing Over," updated January 26, 2020. *Crossing Over | Encyclopedia.com.* Encyclopedia.com. Web. February 7, 2020. <https://www.encyclopedia.com/science-and-technology/biology-and-genetics/genetics-and-genetic-engineering/crossing-over>

Swaab DF, Gooren LJ, Hofman MA. "Brain research, gender and sexual orientation," 1995. *Brain research, gender and sexual orientation. – PubMed – NCBI.* PubMed.gov. Web. September 5, 2019. <https://www.ncbi.nlm.nih.gov/pubmed/7560933>

Swaab, Dick, *Our Creative Brains: How World and Mankind Shape Each Other.* Translated by Liz Waters. 2019. Amsterdam, Atlas Contact.

Swaab, Dick, *We Are Our Brains: From the Womb to Alzheimer's.* Translated by Jane Hedley-Prôle. 2014. London, Penguin Books.

Swaab, Dick F. et al., "Structural and Functional Sex Differences in the Human Hypothalamus," March 1, 2001. *Structural and Functional Sex Differences in the Human Hypothalamus.* Hormones and Behavior 40, 93–98 (2001). Web. September 5, 2019. <https://pdfs.semanticscholar.org/9a43/eba84fb968941b58db76dc2ea02f049fe369.pdf>

Taylor, Lin. "Only five countries give LGBT people equal constitutional rights: research," June 29, 2016. *Only five countries give LGBT people equal constitutional rights:*

research – Reuters. Thomson Reuters. Web. September 23, 2019.
<https://www.reuters.com/article/us-global-lgbt-rights/only-five-countries-give-lgbt-people-equal-constitutional-rights-research-idUSKCN0ZF1IC>

van der Heijden, Godfried W, Maureen Eijpe, and Willy M Baarends. "The X and Y chromosome in meiosis: how and why they keep silent," July 25, 2011. *The X and Y chromosome in meiosis: how and why they keep silent.* Asian Journal of Andrology. Web. February 9, 2020.
<https://www.ncbi.nlm.nih.gov/pmc/articles/PMC373 9570/>

Wikipedia, "Biology and sexual orientation," updated December 31, 2019. *Biology and sexual orientation – Wikipedia.* Wikipedia, The Free Encyclopedia. Web. December 31, 2019.
<https://en.wikipedia.org/wiki/Biology_and_sexual_orientation>

Wikipedia, "David Reimer," updated December 3, 2019. *David Reimer - Wikipedia.* Wikipedia, The Free Encyclopedia. Web. December 13, 2019.
<https://en.wikipedia.org/wiki/David_Reimer>

Wikipedia, "Hermann Henking," updated June 14, 2017. *Hermann Henking – Wikipedia.* Wikipedia, The Free Encyclopedia. Web. February 10, 2020.
<https://en.wikipedia.org/wiki/Hermann_Henking>

Wikipedia, "Xq28," updated September 5, 2019. *Xq28 – Wikipedia*. Wikipedia, The Free Encyclopedia. Web. October 17, 2019.
<https://en.wikipedia.org/wiki/Xq28>

Wikipedia, "Y chromosome," updated January 29, 2020. *Y chromosome – Wikipedia*. Wikipedia, The Free Encyclopedia. Web. February 9, 2020.
<https://en.wikipedia.org/wiki/Y_chromosome>

Williams, Christina L. and Pleil, Kristen E. "Toy story: Why do monkey and human males prefer trucks? Comment on 'Sex differences in rhesus monkey toy preferences parallel those of children' by Hassett, Siebert and Wallen," October 2, 2009. *Toy story: Why do monkey and human males prefer trucks?* NCBI. Web. December 17, 2019.
<https://www.ncbi.nlm.nih.gov/pmc/articles/PMC275 5553/>

Zhou, J. N., Hofman, M. A., Gooren, L. J. G., and Swaab, D. F. (1995). A sex difference in the human brain and its relation to transsexuality. Nature 378, 68–70.

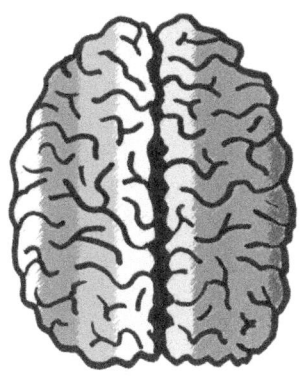

Sign up on our website for a **free pdf article** containing information found on our website: https://notachoice.net/free-articles/.

Please consider leaving a review on Amazon https://www.amazon.com/dp/B07XK8HKQT or https://www.amazon.com/dp/0976323516 or other place of purchase.

Reviews on Goodreads are also appreciated. https://www.goodreads.com/book/show/4807 4070

Thank you
and
Enjoy your day!
-PJ-